HOW TO DREAM A CITY

Plans for a New Chicago from the Students Who Shape It

Foreword by José Olivarez

826CHI

How to Dream a City
© by 826CHI

This book is a work of nonfiction. Names, characters, places, and incidents are products of the authors' personal experiences. Any resemblance to actual events or locales or persons, living or dead, is entirely intentional and emerges from the minds of these authors as truthfully as memory allows.

Cover design: Grace Molteni
Layout design: Wendy Robles

Director of Programs: Maria Villarreal
Publications Coordinator: Waringa Hunja

Proceeds from your purchase of this publication support 826CHI, a non-profit creative writing, tutoring, and publishing center. www.826chi.org

The views expressed in this book are those of the authors and the authors' imaginations. We support student publishing and are thrilled you picked up this book!

First Edition 826CHI 2019 // Printed in the United States by McNaughton & Gunn

Table of Contents

FOREWORD

by José Olivarez

There are many Chicagos, and sometimes those Chicagos share the same moment. Is Chicago the city at Navy Pier where the tourists walk slowly and stop every few feet to take a picture of the ferris wheel? Is Chicago the city of workers rising before the sun to take buses and trains to clean up Navy Pier and make it presentable to the tourists? Do they have a crockpot of ground beef that you can add to your bag of chips at the corner store in your Chicago? Do they have a man selling fruit out of the back of a pick-up truck in your Chicago?

I love the work of this year's Young Authors Book Project from the students at George Washington High School because the authors share their personal visions of Chicago along with their reimaginings of what the city could be. This is a beautiful gift they have given us. In *A Dream Come True*, Esmeralda G. writes "I opened my eyes and the sight in front of me blew me away." That's how I felt reading these poems and essays. I opened my eyes and the sights these authors shared blew me away.

Far from the concrete imaginations that one might expect from children of the city, the young people in this collection show a boundless imagination. In *My Dream Chicago*, Isabella P. dreams of a bus powered by trash provides refuge to the city's homeless. Where does this bus go? The bus flies. Isabella writes, "Once we are in the air, a purple portal shows up in the sky. Once we go through it, we can see mountains, tall, green trees, and water." I do not read this essay as science fiction. While me may not have the technology to produce a bus that uses trash as fuel, we have the resources and ability to help homeless people now. We can protect the green spaces that exist in Chicago.

Chicago is not just one city. It is many cities, and each experience of our beautiful and ugly city is worthy of documentation and praise. I praise these writers because having your work published is a big deal. In these poems and essays they have honored their various Chicagos, their neighborhoods, their families, and themselves. By sharing their stories, the writers in this collection begin a dialogue that encourages all of us to write back. I know that I will get back to my own writing practice thinking of the impossible Chicago I want to make a reality.

This book is a beautiful contribution to the legacy of Chicago writers. Carl Sandburg, Gwendolyn Brooks, Sandra Cisneros, Margaret Burroughs, Kevin Coval, Nate Marshall, Eve L. Ewing, Britteney Black Rose Kapri, Jamila Woods, Erika L Sánchez, Jacob Saenz, H. Melt, and yes, Esmeralda G. & Isabella P & all of their classmates. We are lucky to read their work. We are lucky to belong to Chicago because Chicago's next chapter will be written by these writers.

José Olivarez is the son of Mexican immigrants. His debut book of poems, Citizen Illegal, was a finalist for the PEN/ Jean Stein Award and a winner of the 2018 Chicago Review of Books Poetry Prize. It was named a top book of 2018 by NPR and the New York Public Library. He is the co-host of the poetry podcast, The Poetry Gods, and his work has been featured in The New York Times, The Paris Review, and elsewhere. He is a part of of Costura Creative, a Latinx owned & operated talent agency representing contemporary poets & writers for speaking engagements, readings, workshops, multi-disciplinary collaborations & more.

STUDENT FOREWORD

by Jose C., Laisha F., Benjamin G., Isabella P., and Andrew P.

Writing is always hard. Writing about your life and your dreams for a new Chicago can be almost impossible. We were worried about not being creative enough; we rarely have to use our imaginations for school and we thought maybe they didn't exist.

What helped? Thinking about what we liked and what we wished could be true and what we wanted to see. We had to open up another side of our minds that doesn't get enough use. Reading other people's writing showed us how writing can be fun and weird and futuristic and unusual. We especially recommend reading "Mexican Heaven" by José Olivarez- it made us laugh and think. "Welcome to Unicornopolis" by 826CHI student Isaiah kicked our imaginations into overdrive.

We're ready to put what we think out into the world. We don't get this opportunity very often and we're excited. You'll have different opinions: some of you will love it, some of you will hate it. All we ask is that you reserve judgment until you're done reading and keep an open mind.

We'd like to thank 826CHI for giving us the opportunity to try something new and thank you, the reader, for supporting us. We hope you find more young people's voices to listen to and stand behind. And once you're done reading, go eat a Chicago-style hot dog in our honor.

Stephanie C.

is a 14 year-old from George Washington High School (Grade 9). Stephanie tends to have a very overactive imagination, which tends to lead her to writing and drawing a lot. She enjoys film, painting, and her ever-present ability to memorize song lyrics incorrectly. Her favorite thing to do when she is at home is to sleep, draw, or quietly ignore her irritating older sisters and annoying little brother. She has a deep dislike for any small insects, doing group assignments, speaking in front of large groups, going to school, being in large crowds, and having to keep her voice quiet. Stephanie loves animals, drawing, watching Netflix, reading too many books, and listening to music way too much. When she graduates from high school, Stephanie wishes to go to college and probably pursue a career as an artist.

Seventh Grade

When I was in seventh grade, I had a group of friends. We sat around during lunch talking and laughing. Often I would listen to conversations, left out and desperately trying to be included. One day, they pushed me away from our group. They laughed evilly as I walked away, hanging my head in shame.

I turn around, facing my supposed friends. Quietly, I focus on making them disappear as I close my eyes. I focus on how they made me feel invisible and how I was upset. Suddenly, I open my eyes and smile. A large portal has formed beneath them. They start screaming and crying, scared of what was happening. Finally, they all disappear from sight. To escape, I fly on a bird's wings with a smile on my face. I am going away and being free, leaving cruel things behind. I am surrounded by chirping birds, which sounds like the happiest laughter. The ground is made of cracked pieces of rock, melting under the bright sun into the cool sand underneath. In the sky, the water hangs beautifully in a swirl of blue, clear waves.

But then, I'm awake. It didn't really happen in my real life. The dream is swept away, leaving me awake and missing my blissful dream of defeating bullies. It was just a dream.

Chicago, Chicago

Chicago, a city I call home. Chicago, a city that needs me. Why? Because it does. Chicago needs everyone in a sense, but nobody at all. Right now, Chicago needs me and I'm going to change it.

I'm going to change Chicago by making the city cleaner. Adding more sanitation areas available to everyone, so they may get rid of any garbage or waste safely. It can help our city, especially with how much garbage and other unnecessary items we have in our city that are left on the ground for someone else to pick up. I can change Chicago by getting rid of all the unnecessarily rude and cruel people. Why? Nobody wants to have to deal with rude people at all and their terrible attitudes. What better way than to get rid of them!

Another change could be more dogs! Who doesn't love our four-legged furry friends who bring absolute joy to our faces and love us so dearly? The answer is, nobody besides cruel people. A possible change could be more spaces to do art! Many kids, teenagers, and adults do value art and have the talent to do art, but our beautiful city doesn't offer that many spaces for it. We can open more spaces to do art and offer more art supplies as well, because some may not be able to afford those art supplies that they so greatly need. This can be done by taking old or unused buildings and turning them into awesome, amazing art studios that are filled with any art supplies, plus they could be open for public use! My last change perhaps would be to cut down on school. I mean, seriously! In classes today, students are being taught lessons that don't exactly help them in the future. Instead, we can give students more classes on more important lessons for their future. In addition, students have to be in school for about nine months a year! We can cut down AND give more time to our hardworking students. A real deal!

A change I would also add is more restaurants available to everyone. Everyone likes food, but not everyone can afford the food they want. It sucks and good food should be more accessible to everyone, no matter what their situation.

Angelina K.

is fifteen years old. Angelina attends George Washington High School as a freshman. She has been cheering since first grade. She loves eating chocolate-covered strawberries. She loves to spend a lot of time on the beach. In the future, Angelina wants to go to college.

Vote For Kirby ;)

Chicago needs me and I'm going to change it by making everything more playful. Remember first learning to ride your bike and falling and scraping your knee on the concrete? Yeah, that was rough. We will make streets and sidewalks into hot pink and blue cotton candy. Blue for sidewalks and pink for the streets. So if you fall you will just get a face of delicious cotton candy. The smell will be overwhelming with sweetness to where you'd want to eat the air and there would no longer be that nasty garbage smell. Yes, it will be edible, but only few may eat it. If you did any type of crime you may not eat it, and if you do so you will be put into Gummy Hall. Gummy Hall is where the bad people go. Bad people, like if someone attempted murder or commited murder or even broke into someone's house they'd be sent to Gummy Hall. The bars in Gummy Hall are made up of indestructible red and blue gummies, and if you're really bad, you go into the Candy Cane Chamber. It will be run by the aliens found on Mars.

I will make Chicago safe and fun. If you vote for me, I will raise all pay. The lowest pay you can make is $100 an hour. Now doesn't that sound good? Everyone who lives here will be granted a flying car and an animal of their choice. One more big thing I want to do is have a space program. This program will include two free rides to space and back, and you would get training on how to fly a spaceship. We will hand out half-priced Bloghoused 6000s to certified trained flyers. They're the newest model out right now, with red and white lights to help see when it hits midnight. I know it sounds crazy cool, my friend Mavenly invented them yesterday on his vacation in Pluto. He's one of my favorite Martians, he's 2 feet tall and has a baby face for being almost 290 years old.

Now let's talk about health care. Anything having to do with health will be free. "Oh, I gotta get my teeth done but it's too much." Yeah, you won't ever have to say those words again, because I will help by making it completely free. No more shots in the mouth. We will use marisel, it's not painful. With our new gel we put in your mouth, you will not feel a thing. There are hospitals on every other corner. Each hospital is like a spa. You sit down, they treat your illness, and as they do that you get a whole body massage and face treatment.

"[My space] program will include two free rides to space and back, and you would get training on how to fly a spaceship."

The Story I'm About To Tell You

Anthony R.

is fourteen years old and attends George Washington High School. An interesting fact about him is that he's able to do Stitch's voice from Lilo & Stitch, and he can also pop out a bone from his upper back behind his shoulder. He's also very shy.

The story I'm about to tell you is about a time I acted differently but I really don't remember the whole story. What I do remember is doing something bad to my best friend. After that, a person I was talking to got mad at me and stopped talking to me.

So I took out my wings and flew away to a nice, happy, quiet place to think about what I had done and also to be alone for a while. I stayed in that quiet place for about ten days to see and feel the emotions I gave everyone. I did that for ten days in a infinite loop and one day, I left that place and went back to the world again. Back in the real world, I studied harder and picked up my grades to A's and B's and I felt happy and accomplished. As years went by, I officially graduated college, and I started doing the career I've always wanted to do which is acting, which led me to become a very rich billionaire.

Believe it or not, the people loved me and every time they saw me they would cheer and say, "Anthony, you're so awesome." or "Anthony, can I get a picture with you?" and I would say, "Heck yea! I'd love to take a picture with you guys."

The thing is that there's a big secret I don't want my fans to know, which is that I'm secretly a superhero that stops all the crime in my city. During the day, I'm a rich billionaire but at night, I'm a crime fighter with teleportation, and lightning fast reflexes.

My Street

Chicago needs me, and I'm going to change it by having better neighborhoods like mine. I live by the state line, which is a really safe part of Chicago to live in. Nothing really happens. From time to time a few cars and buses pass by, but most of the time it's really quiet. But one of the problems with the neighborhood is the parking, cause sometimes there's barely space for my parents to park their car. I live in a corner house, so not only is it higher taxes, but my family is also technically supposed to have more parking space. But we only have one tiny spot to park in because cough,cough my neighbor keeps taking up half our spot. I'm like,"Yo, back off and get out of our grill, dog."

But besides having little parking space, it's, like, legit the best neighborhood, because it's for real five blocks away from my friend Adrian's house, Burger King, McDonald's, KFC, Subway, and Pizza Hut. So I'm just saying it's legit the best street to live on. I do miss my old street that was even closer to those places, but it wasn't the safest street, and word on the street is that it's gotten worse over the years. So I'm kinda glad that I moved to a safer neighborhood. But I do kinda miss hearing the train horn every night right before I go to sleep. The sound was so relaxing. The sound actually annoys people most of the time, but it doesn't annoy me, cause it brings nice memories. So if I ever hear the train horn right before I fall asleep, I enjoy it as much as I can before it goes away. That's basically all I can say about my street that I live on.

Well, actually, there's one more thing I could talk about, which is the weather. Because, no joke, if you live in East Side and it's snowing, you better pray. If you have Xfinity as your cable company, I feel you, because every time it snows, their tower goes down, and then you gotta go through the whole day without WiFi. Unless you have data, then you're good. But now that's all I gotta say about my street. But for real, no joke, I hope they stop that tower from shutting down in bad weather. If someone is reading this that can do anything about it, I hope you can feel my pain with that weather thing, but I got nothing else to write, so good day and goodbye.

Alicia B.

is fifteen years old. Her favorite place to go is home and to her bed. What she likes about herself is that she is alway happy. Some things that she dislikes are that people get bullied and that people aren't as nice to each other as they should be. Alicia likes to learn a lot of crazy and interesting things about the world, like science things and sometimes things that have to do with animals. For fun she calls people or plays iMessage games.

Zero Degrees

Yesterday it was zero degrees and my mom wanted me to put on a lot of clothes for no reason when I was only going to be outside for a few minutes. I didn't want to. A few seconds later, she was yelling at me to put them on. I put on my scarf and gloves, then sadly walked out the door.

But then I change my mind and walk back inside to my room and lock the door and take off all my clothes and put my pj's back on and go back to bed, not caring what my mom said.

Chicago Needs Me

Chicago needs me and I am going to change it by having less violence. We should all be kind to each other. In my Chicago, people wake up every day with a smile on their face, saying "good morning" to people and waving.

We should also have flowers—all kinds of flowers, a big bright garden with yellow, bright pink, green, bright blue. Something that makes Chicago really bright so that when you go to outer space and you see Earth, you can see a really bright spot that will be Chicago! Kids can plant up to two flowers and take care of them.

We don't have a lot of nice, bright paintings in stores and libraries. We should have more graffiti on buildings, but respectful graffiti—something that will make someone's day. Graffiti that looks like the Hanging Gardens of Babylon but with buildings having more colors like Mexico and their bright colors but even brighter.

If Chicago had less violence, I think fewer people would be depressed and there would be fewer programs for people with depression, because everybody would be nice and kind to each other.

"My Chicago would be a big island that would be covered with trees, rocks, and animals, and people would use ziplines to go from place to place."

Salvador A.

goes to George Washington High School. He is in the ninth grade. He likes to play sports. The sports that he likes to play are baseball and wrestling. He speaks Spanish and he can speak English. He likes to help out his friends and he likes to hang out with his friends. He likes to spend his time on his phone. When he is not at practice, he likes to spend time with his parents or on Netflix. His favorite foods are tacos and pizza. He likes to play his PlayStation 4. He hopes to join the United States Air Force.

My Chicago

My Chicago would be a big island that would be covered with trees, rocks, and animals, and people would use ziplines to go from place to place. All the homes would be on big trees that are half a mile long. The houses would be connected by a bridge made out of bamboo and wood.

Down on the ground there would be a lot of normal size trees that give out food like apples, strawberries, etc. Some of the old things still remain from years ago, like a bus from the 1960s and a hotel from the 1990s. My Chicago still has a downtown, but that area is overgrown by big trees and lots of water. There is a big waterfall in the center of downtown. That area is for work, and the only job in Chicago is mining. The people dig for gold or for iron. By the big waterfall is a bomb that hit Chicago. The bomb is off limits to the people. Only the mayor and the president can go by the bomb. Everyone has to fend off mutans that live in the shadows—they were the unlucky ones.

When the ziplines are full, people take a fun and better route that is a big and fast waterfall that goes around Chicago. The people have fun because they only have to work two days out of the whole week. The people who live in Chicago know the dangers of leaving their area. Chicago is made up of four parts. We have (area26b), and we have an area that is ruled by mutants called (area24g), then we have (area56t): that area is ruled by monkeys that are mutated. Then we have (area45f): that area has not been explored by the people.

Markanthony P.

is a student at George
Washington High School.

The Lunch Line

The lunch line was taking so long to shorten. It was the first day of 4th grade in a new school. A skinny, tall, frail kid from at least 5th or 6th grade came walking towards me. I looked up to see a freckled face. The shine of his braces blinds me.

"You stupid little kid. Let me cut you or I will deport your family," he said. I stared at him nervously for what felt like forever. I started to sweat immensely. I felt a push from his friends.

I bounce off the green, jiggly, sweet jelly. I quickly catch my balance. My wings spread like a delicate angel.

My Chicago

Chicago needs me, and I'm going to change it by having equal rights for all women and men, heterosexuals and homosexuals, transgender people and others. It would be against the law to discriminate against people who are gay or lesbians. We would have the same wages and income for people who have been mistreated. I would also eliminate all violence and discrimination in the streets, like racism. I would provide a lot of beautiful and modern condos for every person, including homeless people. And all guns would be replaced with fake ones that shoot ice cream (except for the police's guns).

The streets would look so clean and there would be trees everywhere, and beautiful parks for every kid and pet to play in. There would be all varieties of flowers everywhere, and picnics, and abstract art on the pathways. There would less crime. There would be alternative sources for energy, which can provide more food without thieves and robbers taking all of it. This will also avoid all the harmful chemicals like smog harming our environment. It would be so clean that germs wouldn't even be a thing. The only thing you would smell is flowers and beaches. There would also be forests with friendly animals of all kinds.

I'd have beautiful beaches with Mexican restaurants, and kind, swift water. Eco-friendly cars would take over parking lots. On the internet, I saw these cars that had symbols on the back that show that whether the driver is young, old, or middle-aged. I would have that in my Chicago to make it easier to identify someone. There would be new school buildings and repaired ones. I would add a lot of new textbooks and museums.

The people of Chicago can help the city and the environment by recycling and being good citizens. If they follow the laws, and contribute to the political community, they can get rewards like money or medals. For example, if a person votes for the first time, they can get a medal that would represent that they are a first time voter. I would offer all jobs for anything to anyone over seventeen so they can earn a living. I don't like robots who take people's jobs, so there would be no robots in my Chicago.

Marcos R.

is a fifteen-year-old student attending George Washington High School in Chicago, Illinois. His favorite video game out of the many he likes is Delta Rune. He is a very imaginative person and he usually imagines a world that bonds reality with the fantasy of the games, movies, shows, and books he likes. Marcos' life is not fun or goofy; he likes to learn and do things as well as he can to go forward in life. He works with his dad on Saturdays doing maintenance on his dad's working truck. His dream is to become a automotive engineer, fixing, modifying, and restoring cars. He plans to open a dealership/garage to sell old cars and to modify other cars.

World of Something

I was little so I don't remember everything. I was mad, too mad, at something. I felt like I was lost. We were downtown at the Willis Tower. I wanted to go upstairs so badly. I was screaming, yelling, and crying. I got everyone mad at me.

I push everyone away with my mind and they all fall asleep peacefully. I float up each floor, seeing the city at a breathtaking view. I reach the top of the building and jump. I land safely and go home. That night, I dream of a land identical to ours. I am in control. I dream of money for all to buy food that starts with the letter G. Animals come and eat some food while we play fun, unreal games as we swim in a beautiful flooded cave.

I Want To Fix It All

Chicago needs help and I'm going to change it by making it safe. Chicago is not the city it used to be. I want to make it a city where everyone has the chance to grow. I want our children to feel safe. Right now, everywhere we go is outdated: the roads, the bridges, our schools.

I will repair the many draw- and regular bridges that are old and cracking by using any method that they require until they look like new. I will fill up the potholes that are dangerous to the vehicles that cross them everyday with the trusted workers we depend on.

I will make our police force better with the equipment and training to deal with any situation and keep the people who live in danger safe. I will bring opportunities to many who are seeking the chance to succeed in life. I will fund the public schools that need to be fixed and provide the materials to help their students.

I want everyone to have the healthcare they deserve because we all need medical aid. We need a better school system that doesn't only focus on the better schools but on every school. I want a government who spends its money on the city and not on themselves. I want to see this city safer and better, like it used to be. It will take time but it's worth the wait to help the people of Chicago.

Antonio R.

is fourteen years old and he is in ninth grade. He's a basketball and volleyball player and he lives in Chicago. He has a twin named Adrian. He loves to make people laugh and when he plays basketball, it releases stress off his chest.

Better

My Chicago would have safer streets, gun violence reduced, and more homeless shelters. Millions of people die every day from gun violence and guns, but sometimes people get killed from other types of violence. The point that I'm trying to get at is Chicago needs better and safer streets. And in the city in general, people who are poor need homes and food. Sometimes Chicago can't do that for them, maybe because Chicago can't afford it. I feel that we need more money and not just money for the poor, but for everybody. Of course not for the greedy rich people, because they have their money.

My Chicago's name is "Better." This might sound weird, but his full name is Better Reyes Jacob. "Better" stands for a better life for everyone including me and Chicago, "Reyes" stands for my last name, me, my dad, and my brothers, and "Jacob" stands for my little brother and sister. I feel "Better" should have more rights. How about kids having more rights? How about having a voice?

Some rights should be like the age limit for kids to be on their own should be sixteen not eighteen. A lot of kids feel like they should have more rights because they are mature enough, and I feel the same way. Say a kid wanted to live with his aunt and his/her aunt said, "It's okay, you can live with us." Imagine the kid is only sixteen but you have to be eighteen to live with someone else or on your own. That is kind of unfair. Imagine that the family that he/she is living with is abusive. That is pretty unfair to that kid. They could have a better life, live out their fantasies. This has not happened to me, so don't worry.

I feel school should end with ninth grade. I feel that way because everything after that you're not going to really need it in your future life, but you can still have a good future. Plus I feel some people play basketball to sometimes get stress off their chest or just play for fun. Well, I play for both, because it is my favorite sport. I believe that we should have more basketball courts in local areas, but they have to be free. It doesn't matter if it's inside or outside. FREE, period. I hope for more people to do the same as I do and not be couch potatoes. They should try to do what they love or follow their goals/dreams. Because if they don't, they might mess up their lives or be upset at life for not accomplishing their goals.

TAKE A PAGE FROM...
Antonio

"My Chicago's name is *Better*."

Would you rename your Chicago? If so, what would be the new name and why?

Jennifer A.

is a fourteen-year-old freshman at George Washington High School. Jennifer usually goes by Jenny. Jenny loves to play volleyball and has been playing club for three years now. She loves strawberry ice cream, milkshakes, and anything else that contains strawberries. She loves to eat fruits— especially strawberries and grapes rather than chips or chocolate. Jenny loves Mexican food. She loves to help others out as much as she can because she hates seeing others down. She wants to be able to travel the world and go to as many places as possible. She wants to live her life to the fullest.

Most of You Already Know

Most of you already know, but if you don't, I'm a volleyball player. I enjoy playing, and when I'm playing, I'm happy and I don't think about any negative things. I started playing when I was in sixth grade. I never liked it or any other sport. One of my sisters played and since I was tall, her coach, Mr. Flores, asked me if I played and I said no. He told me that I should try it and if I wanted, I should go to their practices. I wasn't sure if I should or not but my dad and sister were trying to convince me to try something new. I ended up going and I was horrible. It was my first time playing volleyball and I was nervous so I played badly. I didn't want to go again and embarrass myself, but my sister told me that it takes practice and that if I keep going, I could get better. I ended up going for the rest of the week, and I improved. I joined the team that year and I kept improving throughout the years playing in elementary. Now I am proud of where I am going with volleyball. I was proud of myself for making varsity as a freshman.

I dream of becoming professional volleyball player and making it far. I know I still have lots of work to do to become a better player. I want to be able to jump so high that I can touch the clouds. When I am on the court, I don't pay attention to who is watching or anything that is not on the court. It makes me feel like I am in my own little world with a few teammates and a ball going back and forward.

My Chicago

Chicago needs me, and I'm going to change it by adding more beautiful tall buildings downtown. If you go inside one of them and go all the way to the top, you can have a really nice view of Chicago. There would also be fun things to do inside of the building like really tall slides, many things to eat, and courts and fields for sports. I would also want to add lights around the trees depending the holiday like red, white, and pink for Valentine's Day, green and red for Christmas, Green for St. Patrick's Day, and all these other cute colors depending on the month.

I would love to have lots of cool and creative sculptures around Chicago where not only are they nice to look at and take pictures of, but they inspire other people and make them feel better about themselves. I want flowers all over the place. Might sound crazy, but yeah. Flowers are just so pretty and some smell really good, and I would love to plant beautiful different types of flowers. I would also plant other nice plants where they can grow to be tall, but not so tall, and where they look cool. There would be lots and lots of delicious food, but mostly Mexican, because who doesn't enjoy Mexican food. There would also be lots of desserts and candy places all around Chicago where you can spend all your money and you wouldn't regret it.

There would be cute dogs that magically appear by you when you want them to, and when you are sad and need someone to cuddle with or even when you are sick with a fever, they would make you feel happy and forget anything sad that ever happened. I would want to build big parks and make a big playground with so many cool and fun things to go on for kids, and I would make soccer fields, volleyball courts, baseball fields, and all the other courts for sports that exist.

My Chicago would have many malls and have so many nice stores like Hollister, Abercrombie, Express, Forever 21, H&M, and all the amazing stores that people like to shop at. In those malls there would also be food courts with places like Dunkin' Donuts, any pizza restaurant, Starbucks, chinese food restaurants, and all the good delicious food. There would be awesome amusement parks and water parks that won't cost a lot of money but are big, and you will have a lot of fun at them with your friends and family.

In my neighborhood there would be big and colorful houses, big, colorful tall trees. Every tree would have colored leaves. One tree can be pink, green, blue, neon orange, purple, yellow, and all the other colors that exist. Same with the houses. They would all be different colors and no house would be the same. One house would be pink, light pink, dark pink, or purple and all the other shades or each color. There would be panaderías, ice cream shops, and little stores around my neighborhood. I want to get rid of lead water and have the freshest water ever. Everyone in my neighborhood would get along and be so nice to each other. They would all treat each other like family. My Chicago would be filled with kindness and respect.

Andy G.

is fifteen years old. He goes to George Washington High School, and he is in ninth grade. He plays soccer, and he is the goalie for the GW soccer team. He hates school because it's boring. He plays video games with his friends and hangs out with his friends. He wants to go to college and study for a career. He also cares a lot about his family.

Andy's Chicago

Chicago needs me and I'm going to change it by making Chicago bigger, better, and amazing. In my Chicago, I'm going to have more security who could watch over the city. Chicago right now is not that safe because there have been gunshots lately. That needs to stop. But I'm also going to make Chicago fun. I will make a maze, and whoever completes it first gets $1 million. In the maze, there will be puzzles, mini-obstacles, and more fun stuff. I'm going to add more pizza places with free pizza so that everybody can eat. I want to build houses for the homeless people, so that they could have somewhere to live or sleep.

I will have water slides in buildings so, instead of using the elevator or the stairs, everyone can use the water slide to get around. I would also let everybody have access to every single video game in the world, for free. Everyone will have robots to make food, so they can just relax.

"I will have water slides in buildings so, instead of using the elevator or the stairs, everyone can use the water slide to get around."

Arturo V.

goes to George Washington High School and is in IB Gym and in honors classes because he's god-like. He loves to play video games on his box. He loves to walk around his block to play some Pokémon Go and catch lots of Pokémon. He also likes food because he's a hungry monster. He is Arturo Vargas. He is amazing and most of all he is handsome. He will be successful. He will dream beyond. He will accomplish.

Down The Stairs

I fell down the stairs about ten times and every part of my body was hurting. Everything was sore from falling all those times. I screamed for help and nobody heard for quite a while but eventually they did hear me and helped me out of my pain.

I dream about wearing shoes that will prevent me from falling down the stairs. Instead of falling, I trip over and land on my bed. A smell of sweetness comes from the cake that falls from the sky and I watching it fall with my very own two eyes.

Chicago Needs Me

Chicago needs me, and I am going to change the city by moving homeless people from the streets and giving them, like, $1,000 to help them find a home and buy food and find a job. I can change the minimum wage and make it $16.75 per hour so people can feed their families. I will also make more jobs available so people can find a job more easily.

I can make schools have vending machines and soda or water machines. There will be no homework, because it stresses out so many kids. Another thing I want to change is better food for school cafeterias with more food to serve to us, because we could be hungry and we wake up super early to go to school. We should suspend people for bullying other kids who have problems by making fun of their looks or their disorders, because that's bad and leads kids or teens to suicide. I want to also stop hunger by giving lots of food and water to the people on the streets who have no money or home.

"I think we would all want a clear sky with a rainbow at all times. Yes, there will be rain and sun, but let's say no to the snow."

Elizabeth G.

is a fourteen year-old student at George Washington High School. Elizabeth's favorite place to be is the Zoo. What she likes about the Zoo is the animals. She likes to see many different species, and all she wants is to see them happy and safe. Something else that Elizabeth likes is going out with her friends. What she likes about it is that she spends time with them and loves having amazing moments with each and every one of them. Elizabeth loves seeing people play soccer or even likes playing herself. She likes anything to do with sports, nature, children, art etc... Her dreams are finishing high school and college and ending off with a good career.

My Chicago

Chicago needs me, and I'm going change it by adding things to it, like more buildings. I would choose buildings, because buildings not only represent more offices, the buildings could also be places where people can donate clothes, money, or hair. We can make it so that everyone in Chicago, starting off as freshmen in high school, gets a job. Or we can build apartments so we can have more homes for people. I would like to make Chicago a cleaner place, without dirt all over the ground, without plastic everywhere. I would stop the gun violence around the community and the violence against women. Everyone should be treated the same . . . with respect. People all over the city should be saying, "Hello, how are you? You look nice today." And the person responding back to them should say, "Why thank you, you look very nice as well!" Now that's a good community, and that's what we should have!

Some ways we can help improve the community are by listening, encouraging each other, being helpful, and saying thank you.

I think my Chicago should be clean and healthy, without drugs or any pollution that kills our plants and trees. We need to get rid of the lead in the water: right now, our water is heavier than lead and clear as Elmer's glue . . . Yes, I might be a bit sarcastic, but that's how I would love my city. I think we would all want a clear sky with a rainbow at all times. Yes, there will be rain and sun, but let's say no to the snow. Snow causes car accidents and leads people to say, "OH NO, WHY DID THIS HAVE TO HAPPEN TO ME!!" We don't need any more harm in here. Stop the damage, harm, danger in my Chicago. We should also create new roads and make them as clean as when you come out of a fresh shower. Forget the old bumpy, messed up, ugly roads. We should have colorful trees all over the place. My Chicago would be a colorful place with red, orange, yellow, green, purple, blue, etc . . . It would smell like grass, flowers, just nature itself . . . It's time for an upgrade.

Make a list or free write:

What do you find beautiful in Chicago?

What do you see in Chicago that others don't?

You can start with the line:

I still think she's beautiful...

Alan M.

is a freshman at George Washington High School. He likes playing soccer and his favorite team is FC Barcelona. His favorite players are Messi and Pelé. Pelé is a legend and Alan wants to be him when he grows up.

Chicago

Well, in my Chicago, I want free subway trains, because I want everybody to enjoy our beautiful town that's really not so bad. I want the train to be like the Hogwarts Express and sell candy and chips and pop and cake. In my Chicago I want free iPhones for the homeless so they can call loved ones or friends who can give them $1,000.

In my Chicago I want every kid to have a PSN card to buy a PS4 and games, or some V-Bucks so they can get some skins for Fortnite. And we can give out some pizza from Route 66 and some cheese sticks from Skyway and some cheese fries, too. And we can have a block party and have some food that my mom makes. She makes *frijoles charros* with salsa, and it's very good.

TAKE A PAGE FROM...

Alan

"We can have a block party and have some food that my mom makes. She makes *frijoles charros* with salsa, and it's very good."

What food would be served at a block party in your Chicago heaven?

Pizza? Tacos? A special family recipe?

"Chicago citizens would feel so much safer that even the air would feel better."

Alberto S.

is a student at George

Washington High School.

The Great Chicago

Chicago needs me and I am going to change it by hiring more officers. I will make sure they sweep the streets constantly. I would also try to stop people from getting unauthorized guns. People will no longer be afraid. They can go out of their houses with no fear of getting shot or attacked.

We can stop people from getting guns by trying to shut down a lot of black markets or the dark web, or we can stop any illegal sellers from selling to gang members or anyone with a criminal record. We can also make it more difficult or be stricter about who gets a gun license. Chicago citizens would feel so much safer that even the air would feel better. It would also feel so much cleaner.

I Wish I Didn't Steal

Man, I wish I didn't steal.
I was like ten years old,
All I did was steal some toys
I got away with it,
After a while
I realized I could get arrested for that,
So instead of going home
I kept those toys,
I wish I Could Have flown back,
On my flying cloud
And flown to the store,
And put all those toys back
Just so I wouldn't feel
The guilt.

Efrain R.

is a fifteen-year-old who lives
on the east side of Chicago. He
likes to go eat at Skyway hot
dogs because their hot dogs
are amazing. Most of the time
he's too tired from school,
so he just gets his missing
sleep and goes to bed when
he comes home. He loves hot
days but not too hot days,
because he says when it's too
hot outside it's a living hell out
there. He also likes windy days
because he says he finds those
days relaxing.

If I Could Run Chicago

If I could run Chicago, I would add more restaurants. I would add more restaurants, because I feel like places like that make Chicago what it is today. When people come here to visit or something, the first thing they do is either go the the Willis Tower or they go eat at the most popular restaurants here, like Giordano's or Portillo's. I would just like to add more of those places to make Chicago even more exciting than any other city in the United States. It would make Chicago more popular, which brings in more people, and with more people comes more money, and with money we can fix Chicago, because right now there's a lot of bad neighborhoods.

Also, if I could run Chicago, I would fix some of the really bad neighborhoods here, cause people living here are living in really bad conditions sometimes. Like gun violence. I would try to get rid of that, because if I don't, more people are at risk of dying in these bad neighborhoods. Also, I would try to fix some of the houses here, cause some are falling apart and people are living there.

Maria R.

is fifteen years old and is a freshman at George Washington High School. She plays soccer. She's a forward and sometimes mid, and a backup goalie when the goalie gets injured. Maria also likes to watch Netflix when she's bored. Maria likes to hang out with her friends when she has nothing better to do. When Maria grows up, she want to be a soccer player, or a doctor, or maybe a nurse.

My Chicago

Chicago needs me and I am going to change it by having no more gun violence. Well, no more guns, period. I feel that if there are no guns, my Chicago would be safer. People would be outside, playing and having fun. Nowadays, people are scared to go outside because people are shooting other people for no reason and that's not allowed in my Chicago. I feel that if that violence is gone, my Chicago would be safer. People could have pocket knifes for protection and if they take the knife out when they don't need it, they go to jail, period. They can't just go around killing people; they can only use their knife when they need it.

My Chicago could also have less time for adults to work. They can have some days off because I know that adults get tired of working and they don't want to go. Adults can have more days off where they don't do anything besides rest. Adults can also stop working when they are sixty-five years old. They can still get money because people can't survive without money.

In my Chicago, everything, especially food, is not as expensive as it is right now. Everyone would eat chicken noodle soup. Then, salad with carrots, little tomatoes, and cucumbers, and pizza (pepperoni, cheese, and sausage). Then you can have your choice of ice cream.

The water from the ocean is pure blue so people can go swimming. Now, people are scared, well, disgusted, because there is garbage. The trees are green, the flowers are out and people have gardens with cut grass. Some people have ponds with fish which are optional. There is no more garbage on the street. My Chicago is clean clean. Also, people get free stuff on Fridays, like shirts that say "Maria's Chicago".

Quick Write

1. What do you love about Chicago?

2. What will love you back in your version of Chicago Heaven?

3. What will be good for you? Good to you?

Ashley L.

is a sixteen-year-old who is in ninth grade at George Washington High School. She's the biggest fangirl in the school and she makes it noticable. She likes to write and draw a lot and she's pretty good at it too, according to her friends. She has a weird thing for unicorns and blobfishes and every animal you can think of. She likes the color black and is tired most of the time. She doesn't like most things that have to do with interacting with people and would rather stay inside. She is very shy and awkward but can be very hyper at times. She wants to work with animals in the future.

Bullies

Once, my friend and I walked to the store to get some things. When we entered the store, I saw some not-so-friendly classmates and man, oh, man. When they saw me, they shouted, "HEY! Emo girl from our non-emo school."

At first, I shrugged it off but then they started to giggle and make more mean comments about my appearance. I started to get a little uncomfortable. As soon as we paid for our things, we were headed out the door but someone said, "BYE, EMO GIRL, see you at school."

I turned around and their lips zipped up and they couldn't speak. Their arms tied up in knots and their legs turned into noodles. I watched with pleasure as they tried to get out of my spell.

Mysterious Chicago

Chicago needs me, and I'm going to change it by making it beautiful and mysterious. I would put gardens of black, white, wine red, and pink roses on every other block. I want troublesome kids running the streets like they own the block. I would put up a statue of a woman with a cloak to represent the mysterious side of Chicago. Instead of guns popping bullets, I want them to shoot kind words. I want the rebels to be rebellious and the calm to stay that way. I would paint the streets in pastel like colors, and I would paint the buildings dark colors to show the dark side of the Chicago. People will be unique in Chicago.

In my Chicago, there will be more trees and life. Stray dogs and cats and the homeless won't need a place to stay for the night because there will be really affordable housing and great shelters. I want the woods to be dark and scary on the outside to the point where people start rumors about them, and once they go in it would be the most beautiful place with life everywhere.

Schools will exist, but they will actually fit students needs in learning. There won't be any homework or tests to see how smart a child is. There will be more hands-on things, like if you're reading a story, make a play of it later. Or if you're doing math, do not just show basic numbers. Doodle around your math problem. There should be more field trips like going out of state or just going to a picnic. Children will learn how to work together but not be so dependant on each other. Yes, they will learn the basics like reading and math, but it'll be more fun. Adults will find the job they want with good pay. There also won't be such thing as animal testing, because my Chicago won't be brave enough to do it. That statement needs no explanation.

Angel M.
is a student at George
Washington High School.

Safe Chicago

Chicago needs me and I am going to change it by getting rid of gun and other violence. I would put more security in stores and other places so it can be safer for the people who are shopping, so they don't get worried if something happens. I would also get more gear for the Chicago police for more safety when a crime occurs. Police cars should have bulletproof windows and doors so when they have shootouts, the bullets get stopped by the window glass. They should also have bulletproof wheels so they won't get shot off and the cop won't lose control of the car and crash and hurt other people. Then, the police can be safer than ever and don't have to worry.

Nathan F.
is fifteen years old
and attends George
Washington High
School. He loves
to play games and
enjoys to work out.
He also likes to live
stream and post it on
YouTube.

Chores

My mom got mad at me
because I didn't do the chores
because I was distracted by
my game. When she got home,
she asked for the towels and I
had forgotten to wash and dry
them.

*But she didn't realize that I hit
one million Twitch followers and
YouTube subscribers which made me
happy and made me popular and
famous.*

Ariana C.

is fifteen years old.
Ariana is a freshman
at George Washington
High School. Her favorite
place has to be California
because all of her family
is there and they are fun
to hang out with. Ariana
is sometimes really
sarcastic and also clumsy.
Ariana's dream is to be a
nurse like her aunt.

My Unique Chicago

Chicago needs me and I'm
going to change it by making
every gun in Chicago a Nerf
gun. Chicago will be where the
rich people give some of their
money away to the homeless. I
want Chicago to have no more
racism. I want people to have
respect for others and not be
mean to them. There are more
things that Chicago needs but
the city really needs to focus on
the people because they are the
future. They are important.

"The city really needs to focus on the people because they are the future. They are important."

Laurie A.

is a student at George
Washington High School.

The Angry Trolls

When I was in Tennessee, there was a party for a wedding. When I got there with Josh, it was really loud. I'm not a party person, so I'm not a fan of loud music.

When I look up, there is a troll nibbling at the roof. His face is fire-red. Trolls hate loud music. I look at the roof again and all I see is the dark, star-filled sky. I look around for the ugly troll. When I find him, he is nibbling at the speakers. The music sounds terrible. It is just static coming out, and people start to notice. Everyone screams and runs for their lives. I just stare at the trolls, smirking.

My Unique Chicago

There are many flaws and impurities in Chicago, and there are also many places to make memories. Chicago can be a beautiful place when it wants to be. Other days, not so much. There is violence and littering, but there are also weddings, and much more.

A thing I would change in Chicago is the violence. Many people get hurt every day, whether it is from a gun or from bare hands. Instead of guns, I would give everyone a loving animal, so instead of spreading violence they would be spreading love. As an example, if you are a person who relies on affection, a cat or dog would be great for you because they are loving and affectionate animals.

Another thing I would change in Chicago is the amount of homeless people. When I'm downtown every road I go onto there is a homeless person, which isn't good. To lessen the amount I would build more homeless shelters so that they have a place to stay and get fed instead of staying in the heat or the cold. No one deserves to be living on the street. I would also make fundraisers for the homeless where they would get to go places and have free food given to them like it's a party.

I would also change how schools are made in Chicago. I would help CPS schools get funded more so they can get newer books, more programs for kids, and a better environment. At these schools I would put huge vending machines that carry drinks and snacks and a huge courtyard filled with fun things to do. A lot of the books we have in school are pretty old and written all over and torn up. I would fund the schools so they'd get fresh, clean books. A lot of the school buildings are filthy and run down. I would get the schools cleaned up and get renovations done to make the schools cleaner and safer for everyone. The buildings will look spotless, brand new, and beautiful. They'll have a modern touch with lots of cool technology made for learning.

What's the perspective or lens shift that you want Chicago to change or focus on?

Make a list or free write to brainstorm answers to this question.

You can start with the line:

I'm going to tell you what's unfair in Chicago...

OR

Things need to be different in Chicago...

Nadia P.

is fourteen years old and
goes to George Washington
High School. She lives
and grew up in the South
Side of Chicago. She loves
playing volleyball and
binge watching Netflix on
the weekends. She is super
tall and loves pineapples.
She likes to have fun in the
summer but not any other
season because her birthday
is in August. Right after
high school she is going to
the Marines. She gets the
shivers when somebody
scratches clothing. She loves
being alone in quiet spaces
just to think.

I'm Sorry, Mom

I wish I hadn't acted a certain
way toward my mom after she
tried to help me. She tried to
help with my homework but I
yelled at her and told her, "If I
needed help, I would ask for it.
LEAVE ME ALONE!" My mom
said, "Oh, okay," and went back
to her room, closed the door,
and lay down.

*When I needed help, I asked the
math giant to do my homework
for me. He gave me a piece of
lettuce that made me the smartest
mathematician in the world. I stood
at the top of a really tall beanstalk
screaming all the math formulas and
equations from my homework and,
in the snap of a finger, they would be
solved.*

My Chicago

Chicago needs me and I'm going to change it by making it the most fun city in the world. The transportation will be roller coasters instead of trains. Instead of the sound of people honking their cars and yelling at each other, you will hear music blasting that the adults hate. It will be a teens' world. No more adults, just teenagers making important choices. Instead of cars and big polluting trucks, everyone will have an electric bike like Elastigirl had in Incredibles 2. Every teen will have a big mansion with their own private chef making their favorite food. The chefs will of course be adults. They won't talk, because they just tear us down when they do.

Instead of Buckingham Fountain spewing water, it will spew pure Fruit Punch— the gas station brand, because the taste is just the best thing in the world. Everyone will have a gold horse for the horse riding contests held in Soldier Field. Everyone will wear designer brands like Dior, Chanel, Fendi, Gucci, and Cartier. The sky will be dark all the time and the hot summer weather will be in the air at all times because summer at night is another dimension. Every girl will have what they want and be the best at what they wanna do. Every boy will have the freedom to do what they want to do and the money to get what they want to get.

Instead of guns, there will be water guns. Instead of knives, there will be balloon animals. Instead of lies, there will be cotton candy you can fall on when you get hurt. There will be no more death. There will just be life and happiness in the air. That smells like the perfume Pink Sugar from Ulta. There will be no cats and dogs, because they smell everything up and ruin relaxation. Everyone will have 1 million dollars to blow, but they won't really need it because everything is free. People will be able to go to the grocery store, take what they want, leave, eat, take it, eat, leave. It's a never ending cycle. There will be no rules or cops, because they ruin the fun.

There will be speakers on every street corner blasting the song "Pop Out" by Polo G, "187" by Lud Foe, and "Swervo" by G Herbo. Everyone has the same music tastes. No more 45th president, because he's a weirdo. Politics are not a thing because they're boring. No more seasons, because every day is summer, but Christmas is still a thing. No more time or clocks, because they cause stress. No more school, because it's holding us back. It's holding us back because they swear they know 100 percent what we want to do. They don't let us make our own choices. All day everyone sits around doing what they want. They go on walks, they go for drives if they still have a car, they go to the beach, they go shopping, they just do what they wish.

"One or two times a month, we would throw a block party and everyone who is able to will come. There will be basketball hoops and grills and bean bag games and cotton candy for the kids and there will be a DJ."

Andrew A.

is sixteen years old and is a freshman at George Washington High School. Andrew's favorite team is the Lakers because Lebron James and Lonzo Ball are on the team. He likes to play soccer, he loves vanilla ice cream from DQ, and he wants to be a basketball player in the NBA.

My Chicago

In my Chicago, I would want there to be peace. No one needs violence. People will know one another, because one or two times a month, we would throw a block party and everyone who is able to will come. There will be basketball hoops and grills and bean bag games and cotton candy for the kids and there will be a DJ. Also, Trippie Redd will be there. And the people will get to know each other by finding things that they have in common, like sports. The moms will get together and share their recipes, and people are down. Some other people like your neighbors will be there to help you if you need it.

Benjamin G.

is a fifteen-year-old freshman at George Washington High School. Benjamin likes to play and hang out with his friends. He likes playing online on his Xbox. He becomes easy friends with some people but not all of them. Benjamin is a Mexican-American who can understand more Spanish than he can speak. Benjamin watches anime and is currently watching Tokyo Ghoul, Naruto Shippuden, and Dragon Ball. Benjamin plays Rainbow Six Siege, Call of Duty, etc. He used to be a hardcore Christian so he couldn't play games, listen to music, or make many friends in the outside world. He was in an undivorced family but now lives with his mother. This helped him play games and listen to music and make more friends. Benjamin wants to be a videogame designer.

My Perfect Chicago

What I want to happen in Chicago is for it to be safer, cleaner, and more sustainable. I want everybody to have an unlimited amount of money so people won't have to kill, rob, or join a gang for money. If they don't do any of those things, the crime level will drastically decline, and there will be cures for every sickness so people with mental disorders won't have to suffer. People could be whatever they want; they can be a superhero or just another person—it is up to the person. I want not one section of Chicago to live in poverty and pollution—what I want to do is gather all the trash and make plastic streets that can last longer than normal roads. Also, I will demolish all factories that produce smoke and try to get rid of buildings that produce pollution.

In my Chicago, it is going to be peaceful and advanced. One side of Chicago will be the city; the other side will be an infinite world filled with trees, mountains, rivers, and oceans that haven't been touched by mankind, but you can see people in the distance. In the infinite world, you can see the stars at night and you can watch the city glow. You could also interact with animals and talk to them. You can also choose where you want to live—you can live underwater without being harmed and you can live near a volcano or in one without being hot or harmed. You can also generate yourself a house in the wild as long as you don't harm nature or people. You can also have a house in the sky and lay on the clouds. You are going to be able to make friends with animals and you can become friends with anyone. No one will judge you because no one will have the ability to judge someone. At a specific location, you can play the games you want and actually be in them, but you won't get hurt in anyway. You will also be able to play with friends and have a wonderful time. You can make your own movies and watch movies in the sky, but it doesn't affect everyone—you are the only one able to see it. You can lie down and look up so the movie is kinda like the Hunger Games death icon.

In the city there are big see-through plastic tubes that cars can ride in like a freeway, and there are hovering cars that have no wheels. The city is kinda like the TV show Dragon Ball—there are capsules, and if you push the button on top and throw it, you can get a vehicle—even a tank—but for a tank, you need a tank capsule. In the tubes you can see advanced skyscrapers and normal ones, as well some with bright, vibrant colors. For example, there is a big skyscraper that is a vibrant yellow that has a good mixture of dark yellow as well. Once you get to open areas you can see people running, and you can see mothers with strollers and babies inside, smiling because of the small fluffy toy. There are no signs or traces of homeless people and no signs of drugs on the streets. There are no homeless people because all of the homeless people have homes, and there are no drugs because there is no use for them. Everybody is happy and no one can get an illness. Everybody is immortal and since the city is never ending, everybody can fit in the city, so you can have as many children or pets as you want.

Rogelio R.

is a fifteen-year-old freshman at Washington HS. He plays and helps younger kids with football. He stays in the east side of Chicago and works. He doesn't focus on all the internet woofin'.

At Work

One time, I was at work and I got stuck with all the boring stuff. I had to clean the whole store. In the back, the boxes were all over the place and there was food on the table and in the front, the phone cases were all over the place and I had to put the signs out. I still did my nine hour shift at the register. All through that day, everybody that walked in made me angry for some reason and I was mad because I had to clean the store in the morning.

A spider came and told me to go home because my day was done. I didn't want to leave though. I wanted to keep working more hours to get a better paycheck. The spider kept telling me to go ahead and leave but I had only done a nine hour shift and I wanted to do a full eleven hours because I had nothing to do later on. As I worked, the spider kept bothering me and wouldn't let me do my job correctly. I got mad and I threw a newspaper at the spider. He dodged it and got mad at me. He told me that I should leave before I do an eleven hour shift because the streets would be dark but I got mad at him for trying to tell me something good.

The spider used to be a bad spider but he wanted to be better so he decided to help people and he came to help me. The spider had a bad life and when he came to me that day, I pushed him away and ignored him so he left. I ended up working the full eleven hours like I wanted to but the streets were dark when I left like spider had told me. I almost lost control of my truck and nearly crashed into a semi-truck but swerved and got back in control. When I got home, I thought, Damn, that spider was just trying to help me. I been down that road and I wanted to do better. I should've just helped him while he helped me.

Chicago Is Good The Way It Is

Chicago is good the way it is, but we should have fewer cops and more business owners. Chicago needs more athletic sports in bad neighborhoods (use basketball courts for competitive games with sponsors). Jobs (cooks, restaurants) for younger people to stay out o the way of gang violence. Chicago needs racism to END: not every Mexican is illegal and not every black person is armed.

Most people in Chicago are in bad neighborhoods. We could be the ones to turn that around. We can't keep everyone from the streets, but we could help and guide them the right way so mistakes aren't made. A lot of the gang members want a way out and we could help and provide for the young and for the people that want to do better with themselves. Chicago needs more restaurants so more young people could work and get out of the streets, because other rivals got no aim and will hit anybody. Chicago should put more money into school sports. A lot of people here came from the bottom, but many didn't. We could help our people in Chicago get out of the hood and get into a better lifestyle. I speak for the people in Chicago when I say I'm tired of hearing gunshots that wake me up out my sleep. I'm tired of the flashbacks. I want a better way, and we're gonna make it.

Growing up in wrong neighborhoods can really mess with your head, and not many people think of getting out of it. Imagine walking out of your house and every day you see a group of eight people on the corner throwing gang signs at everybody. You want to help the younger people do better, but they turn to that life like others did because there are only three ways out, and that's dead, in prison, or making it in life.

"Improvement of all the schools in Chicago means better buildings, better supplies, and better desks. I also want the funding for CPS used for the improvement of the infrastructure of the buildings. . . . Your children will now be able to live in a better, improved Chicago."

Christopher W.

is a fifteen-year-old author from Chicago, Illinois. He is a freshman and he attends George Washington High School. His hobbies are playing basketball and football. He also dabbles in horticulture and enjoys the outside. He is a big smartass and always has something to say. He has a RBF (hmu for what it means) but is usually in a good mood. His goal in life is to live long enough to be that old guy who reads upside-down newspapers on his porch and drinks iced tea and criticizes the youth. His dream is to be rich enough to buy his mother a house but still be able to flex on those who wish to see him do badly. He doesn't know what a bruin is.

A New Chicago

Chicago needs me and I'm going to change it by making it safer for people to walk out of their houses. No one wants to be scared to walk to the corner store, and everyone should be able to take their kids outside. First, guns would be swapped out with paintball guns. No more mothers will lose their sons to gun violence. There would be way more trees in our neighborhoods, making our air a lot better and raising the house prices. Also, I will be adding more parks with outside courts to the community and improving the indoor courts we have.

All students will be protected leaving schools and won't be harmed. I will also add more sport programs and leagues in my neighborhood to keep kids off the streets and into something productive. I will also legalize marijuana, keeping small time offenders out of prison and saving taxpayer money. I will add more marijuana dispensaries to calm the nerves of uptight people and to provide medication for those who need it. I will also have public transportation that instantly transports the passengers to the next stop. I will give electric cars to every homeowner. Also, all homeless kids will have the best shelters to go to. I will have better restaurants like the nice ones in California.

I would like better training for the police and to have officers who are from the neighborhood they are patrolling. There will be no more officers from the North Side in the East Side. Improvement of all the schools in Chicago means better buildings, better supplies, and better desks. I also want the funding for CPS used for the improvement of the infrastructure of the buildings as we have many leaks and ceilings are falling apart. Your children will now be able to live in a better, improved Chicago. I will also push for more libraries in the area to provide a place for those trying to learn.

There will be more Capri's Pizza's built all over Chicago. I think that better restaurants will provide jobs for younger people in school. There will also be more hospitals built in the area; we are in high demand of these and they will benefit us greatly. I will also outlaw cyber-bullying. If you bully someone, they have the legal right to beat the crap out of you. A lot of potholes will be repaired. Bridges will be fixed and improved. It's gonna be a good Chicago.

Mayra H.

is fifteen years old and goes to George Washington High School. Mayra has been living in Chicago since day one. Mayra likes to play volleyball with her family. Mayra likes to eat Mexican food. Mayra likes to go to the movies. She likes the popcorn and the candy there. She only likes getting limon and mango ice cream at the ice cream store. She loves math. When she grows up she wants to be a math teacher. That is her future goal.

Chicago Needs Me

Chicago needs me, and I'm going to change it so that you have a chance to live longer. It's going to have nice, bright colors for you to feel happy. There will be lots of sweet and kind animals and very very tall trees. For example, there will be blue spruce trees and nice sunsets for everyone to see. Downtown you can see a sunset at 2:30 p.m. and then there will be another sunset by Calumet Park at 4 p.m. Chicago is going to be a magical city for you to live in. The parks won't just be plain colors like green, brown, and gray. The parks are going to be very colorful with bright pink, light green, and lots and lots of wonderful colors for you to see while taking a nice long walk. People won't be homeless. They will have a little place to live.

Chicago needs me, and I'm going to change it so that if you get lost, you will have a map pop up right in front of you. If you say, "I need help and I need it now," it will give you directions to the location you need to get to. The food is going to be very good. There are going to be lots of Mexican restaurants. I will find a way to make downtown very nice and pretty. If you're moving from one place to another, come down to Chicago. You will love it even if you have kids that are little. There are different types of playgrounds for different ages.

"Downtown, you can see a sunset at 2:30 p.m. and then there will be another sunset by Calumet Park at 4 p.m. Chicago is going to be a magical city for you to live in."

Quick Write

Write a poem or make a list where every line begins with:

My Chicago is...

My Chicago is...

My Chicago is...

My Chicago is...

My Chicago is...

My Chicago is...

Kevin M.

(grade 9) is a fourteen-year-old male who lives in Chicago. Kevin's favorite place is his home. He loves exploring the past and is glued to his bed. His favorite animals are dogs. Kevin loves making other people laugh, making them happy, and having fun. He is a very relaxed and funny person.

Chicago needs me and I'm going to change it by. . .

-reducing the crime rate.
-ending homelessness and giving money out everybody who truly needs it.
-making sure gun violence rates drop severely.
-abolishing poverty and making sure people have a bit to eat at night.
-legalizing medicinal marijuana or just marijuana in general

People no matter what gender, race, and sexuality will be treated equally.

Isabella P.

is fourteen years old. She goes to George Washington High School. She is a very goofy person who likes to laugh a lot and at anything. She loves movies and watching them on Netflix. She plays softball; it's one of her favorite sports. She loves skincare and spending time with kids.

My Dream Is Chicago

Chicago needs me and I'm going to change it by helping make the streets safe for the people living there. If I were the mayor, I would bring a fun bus for the people on the streets. It would work by going to each street in the city one day at a time. Once the homeless people got on, they would feel clean and warm because it can be really cold outside. Inside the bus, they see very bright and warm colors. As they walk in, they can swap their old clothes for new clothes. As they walk toward the back of the bus, they get their own magical book bag to take back to the city. In this magical book bag, there is an endless amount of food and water. After they get a lot of goodies, they take a seat on a massage chair that is powered by juice. This would a different type of juice, made out of organic trash so we can also help our city to clean up. If there is trash on the streets, the bus would pick it up from the bottom. Once we are ready to roll, we go to a field and the bus switches over from drive to fly. Once we are in the air, a purple portal shows up in the sky. Once we go through it, we can see mountains, tall green trees, and water. As we get closer to the ground, you can hear music that makes you feel good.

When we land, there is a big entrance to welcome everyone. As we get off the bus, everyone leaves their stuff because they will come back. Since it wasn't a long ride, everyone is happy to be there. From a distance you can see a carnival flashing bright lights that draw everyone's attention.

TAKE A PAGE FROM...

Isabella

Design a machine that tackles several different concerns in the city.

Isabella's bus addresses homelessness, hunger, and littering.
What will yours focus on?

"Las personas no serán más discriminadas por tener diferencias."

Jennifer L.

tiene 14 años de edad y estudia en George Washington High School. Le gusta leer comics y también le gusta practicar gimnasia, y ballet. Le gustan las matemáticas. Hace dos años que vino de México; está muy interesada por aprender el inglés. Su nacionalidad es americana, pero desde pequeña vivió en México. En su futuro piensa ser ingeniera/pediatra. Su gran deseo para el futuro es viajar por todo el mundo.

El Gran Cambio

Chicago me necesita y voy a cambiarlo para ayudar a personas que son tan pobres que a veces no tienen nada de dinero para poder comer, a veces tienen que aguantar el frío porque no tienen donde dormir y duermen en la calle. Que las personas que viven en la calle, tengan un hogar. Haré una organización para que no haya más discriminación de estatus socioeconómico, porque lo único que hace CPS es separar a las personas que tienen dinero y a las que no tienen, o sea por estatus socioeconómico. En esta ciudad no quiero más violencia, ¿Por qué tiene que haber tanta violencia? Parece que es algo en el que se les paga para que lo hagan. Muchas personas pierden a sus seres queridos por culpa de tanta violencia; no es agradable, es como que te llaman y te dicen que alguien de tu familia está muerto porque alguien le dio un balazo. Te sentirás super mal, ¿verdad?.

Como la semana pasada, hubo un evento violento por el barrio donde vivo, en la 106 street en el East side, un hombre le disparó a una mujer. Cuando salí de la escuela había policías por dondequiera y había un helicóptero muy cerca por aquí en este barrio.

Cambiaría la mentalidad de las personas, porque algunas personas no tienen la mente bien, están muy locas, y a veces no piensan lo que están haciendo y por eso cometen cosas aunque no quieren que pasen. Cambiaría su mentalidad también porque hay personas tan racistas; es desagradable que discrimines a alguien que no es como eres tú, por ser de otro color, tener otro idioma, etc. Ya no es como tú, todos somos humanos , solo con diferentes rostros. Como cuando yo tenía 7 años, tuve que ir a vivir a California porque mi mamá tenía que trabajar, pero a mí no me gustó para nada. Allí no entendía ni una sola palabra, y los que eran mis compañeros siempre se burlaban de mí o me decían cosas que ni podía entender, pero me sentía muy mal. Yo no quiero que eso les pase a los niños, por eso voy a crear una organización donde, desde pequeños, a los niños se les enseñen a respetarse, para que se vean de la misma manera.

Y ahora como Chicago tendrá un gran cambio, no habrá violencia, no habrá más personas muertas por error. Tampoco habrá personas en la calle; cada una de esas personas va a tener a lo menos un cuarto en donde dormir y sin tener que pasar el frío en la calle. Las personas no serán más discriminadas por tener diferencias, y mucho menos los niños en las escuelas. Todos en Chicago van a estar felices por el gran cambio que va a pasar.

Andrew P.

(probably a freshman when you're reading this) is a fun-loving old man trapped in a fourteen-year-old's body. His dream career is writing for TV shows and becoming a cartoonist and animator. His favorite things in the world are thousand-year-old relics like as rock and metal music, Mr. Pibb Cherry Soda, his parents, and everything that has to do with Transformers and giant robots/monsters. The cartoons he watches, much like the humor he likes, vary from extremely corny puns to mind-meltingly offensive jokes. That helped start the idea in his head that he wanted to entertain and make people happy as a life goal.

Retold

It was another Thursday afternoon at school, just like a whole bunch of the weekdays scattered throughout months, with a bunch of the "cool" kids telling me how stupid I was one at a time every five minutes. Sometimes it didn't phase me, but there were bad times when they used the word retard.

One time, when the "coolest" and stupidest kid of the bunch kept treating me like I had an IQ of 5, I stood there and *started to roast and make fun of him in about ten different languages, only two of which he could understand. I grabbed him by the belt and ran down the stairs at 50 m.p.h. pushing everyone back and making papers swirl around me, and threw him in the kindergarten class so he could learn a lesson in manners from the seven year olds. Then I ran back to class just in time to finish my work.*

Perfect Chicago

For me to make a perfect Chicago, I really don't need to change much. It's an amazing city, but it's got huge bits and pieces of things wrong with it that make you want to shout, "Why am I still living here again?" Poverty, gangs, and gunshot bangs have probably happened at least once anywhere you go in Chicago. Yeah, I don't think I want to keep that around while I'm the leader around here.

Let the people who actually need guns keep them, like anti-racist cops and a couple of security guards. Make a new type of rehab, but instead of people who have taken part in drugs, it's a bunch of guys who have been a part of gangs who get taught about how much better and happier their lives could be when they get rid of their "savage life." Un-teach them everything that they learned about being a gangster. Teach them how not to steal, how to not kill anyone they've got beef with, how not to start any beef to begin with, and finally have a happy life.

Have the Treasurer of Chicago be somebody who went through poverty as a kid and wants to help citizens of Chicago who are going through the same struggles, and pretty soon, there won't be that many people who need help.

The hood won't be a place where people dread living in because of all the violence happening there anymore. Instead it will be a place where people of hundreds of different races are all living together, yet even with a neighborhood population in the thousands, everyone knows everybody in the neighborhood, just like the old days in the ghetto. Everybody in the neighborhood treats each other like one massive, insanely huge family because of how many wild and good times they've had together. There will be parties and gatherings and cookouts with everybody you know within about five miles of the hood. It will be a place where so many different kinds of people live. Blacks, Latinos, Muslims, Indians, and like, five white guys, tops.

And the rest of the city won't be much different. The only real difference is that there won't be houses spanning for a couple of blocks. Instead it will be what downtown is like now. Stores and family-owned restaurants and corner stores as far as the eye can see. Houses will be replaced with apartments and college dorms with people living their best lives in the city, trying to make their future bright and living the American Dream in a city that's probably 80% Hispanic.

Titanic thousand-foot tall goliaths of buildings will surround the city to give you the feeling that only big cities can give. The Sears tower is given its proper name. Parks and food trucks will go for miles until they reach mountains and hundreds of acres of trees and forests only about 100 feet away from the rest of the city. Chicago has become the new happiest place in the world, and Disneyland can just barely compete for the title.

Retellings

inspired by Eve L. Ewing's *Electric Arches*

Make a list:

1. An argument you didn't win/wish you had said something different

2. A time when you were told/made to feel like you didn't belong

3. A time when you wish you had acted differently

Your turn:

1. Pick an event from your list that you want to do-over.

2. Write out the WHOLE scene first. Even how it originally ended.

3. THEN - find a place where you want to press pause to change the ending!

4. Write your new ending - with magic! Make it fantasy - Make it up as you go!

Osvaldo C.

is fourteen years old. He goes to George Washington Elementary School. He likes to play basketball. His favorite team in basketball is the Bulls. He likes to go home and eat because he gets hungry. He likes to hangout with his friends and his girl. He wants to have a lot of money in the future to have nice things and also to help other people out—especially his family.

Chicago Needs Me

Chicago needs me and I'm going to change it by making it a bit bigger just to put in more beaches and more islands. I would have my own castle with my own birds that are trained so if they leave they would come back. My Chicago would also be like summer but with cool wind, so that it could feel nice. I would change all the crime into no more crime in Chicago. Also, in my Chicago I would make it so that everyone is immortal, and also I would make everyone young, like around in their twenties. I would also make more public soccer fields so that everyone can meet each other and go and have fun. Also I would have my friends live in my castle and we would all have the best monitors and consoles.

I would have a lot of nice buildings, a lot of nice cars, and everything in the world would be free so we could buy all the V-Bucks in the world. Also everywhere I'd go it would rain money, so if there is anyone near me they would be able to get money as well. The other people's houses in the city would not be as big as mine, but they would be mansions, because everyone needs to be in a nice home so that they could feel comfortable and safe. Anyone can be on the island as long as they aren't any danger to it. There would be a lot of water like pools and the ocean is around, but there aren't any storms or stuff that can mess up the island.

"I would make it so that everyone is immortal, and also I would make everyone young, like around in their twenties."

Make a list of 2-5 each.

- Your favorite things about the city.

- Your favorite places to go.

- Your favorite food.

- What's the most Chicago thing?

- Where is home for you?

- Where do you belong?

Grace P.

is fourteen years old. She lives in Chicago and she attends George Washington High School. She likes to eat ice cream, her favorite movie is Tres Metros Sobre el Cielo, and she likes to go walking with her friends. A place that she would like to go is Colombia.

Lo que yo haría para mejorar Chicago sería. . .

-más seguridad para las personas, niños y niñas para que cuando salgan sientan la seguridad de afuera
-lugares para que las personas indigentes tengan un lugar para que duerman, coman, y se bañen
-más agua, árboles, y más naturaleza en partes de Chicago.

Vanessa T.
is a student at George
Washington High School.

My Brother

A time I wish I had done
something different was when
my brother was making fun
of me. While he was laughing,
I got up and started slapping
him. He kept blocking me, and
he put his elbow up. My arm
ended up hitting his elbow. My
arm hurt a lot for about two
days.

*After it stopped hurting, my arm
and everything I had turned purple.
My hair turned rainbow colors.
I decided to take revenge on my
brother for hurting my arm. I used a
magical spell on him and a dragon
appeared out of nowhere and took
my brother and me. The dragon
dropped off my brother and trapped
him in a magical egg. I was finally
able to defeat my brother.*

The New Chicago

Chicago needs me and I'm going to change it by making the environment cleaner. The cars won't run on gasoline. Trees won't be cut down as much, and there won't be as much trash on the ground. There will be recycling bins on every street or corner. The zoos will be bigger to hold more animals and keep them safe. The parks will have more trees and plants, and animals will be there to visit like butterflies and other insects. Every park will have a fountain in the middle, so people can toss coins in for good luck if they want to. All the animals can talk, so people will understand them better. Everyone will have an animal companion.

Mythical creatures like unicorns and dragons will exist. At night, people will be able to see the stars and the sky will look like space. Buildings and houses will stay the same, and factories won't have smoke coming out from them. People don't have to worry about bills—they won't exist. People will go to school once a week for four hours, and they can choose to go in the morning or in the afternoon. Everyone will be able to afford a home—houses won't be so expensive.

TAKE A PAGE FROM...
Isabel

"I want to follow my dreams like being a fashion designer, cosmetologist, or photographer. I want kids to be like me, following their dreams."

What dreams would you follow if there was nothing standing in your way?

What new job would you invent, like Isabel's designer-cosmetologist-photographer?

Isabel R.

(Grade 9) attends George Washington High School In Chicago. Isabel is fourteen years old. Isabel loves chips and all those really good snacks. She loves to eat in general. She is a very nice, generous, fun-to-be-with, and loyal girl. She wants to study cosmetology; she is really interested in makeup and hair. Isabel likes to play volleyball and likes swimming. She dislikes seafood and fake people.

What I Want in Chicago

Chicago needs me and I'm going to change it by following my dreams and believing in myself. I would let kids in school have more time in recess. I want to follow my dreams like being a fashion designer, cosmetologist, or photographer. I want kids to be like me, following their dreams. Every kid has the choice to do what they want in life, and I prefer for kids to be what they want and to believe in themselves. Also for adults, it's never too late to go to college and be what they wanted for their entire lives. Maybe their parents couldn't afford it or they just didn't feel good about it, but it's never too late for adults.

I want people in Chicago to be who they really want to be, and I want them to believe in themselves. Even if it's too much to handle like stress and anxiety, all you need is to believe in yourself and in what you want to be. Just because you graduated high school doesn't mean that you need to stop doing what you want to be in life and what you always wanted to be. Make yourself proud, make your peers proud, and make your family and parents proud. Let them know that what age you are in college doesn't mean anything, college doesn't have an age. I also want poverty to not even exist. People probably didn't think or want to do anything when it got to that point of picking of what they actually wanted to be in life. It's not their fault—it's no ones fault.

Alejandro H.

is a fifteen-year-old student at George Washington High School. Alejandro's favorite place is Cal Park. He's favorite thing to do is to play soccer in the park. Alejandro dislikes when the streets of Chicago are not clean. Alejandro wants A's and B's on his report card. Alejandro likes to make people laugh and likes to have a good and fun time with other people. Alejandro's dream is to go to a good college.

My Chicago

Chicago needs me and I´m going to change it by listening to the most needed people from here. I would make people feel safe in Chicago by making the border from Chicago to Indiana safer because guns are being passed from Indiana to Chicago. I would not put up a wall or anything like that because that can harm the animals from the area. I would have more police force at the border and I would put more cameras over at the ends of Chicago.

I am not saying that it's all on Indiana—it's on Chicago as well, because of all the gangs in our area and how we let them do transactions with each other. Making these transactions stop would be almost impossible, but if we try, we may be able to make a difference in our streets. People would be more confident in the streets—kids get to play more often in their parks, and people can actually walk on the sidewalk in the morning. That's not all it would impact—it would also impact our jobs, and the reason behind that is because the best and biggest gangs are only big because of guns and drugs—the more the guns, the better the gang. Now, if they have no guns with them, the more afraid they are, and the more they turn to real jobs because they realise they're in even more danger because they have nothing to defend themselves with. But that is just an idea.

Chicago needs more nature around the city. I would make a project for the city and the people of Chicago—we would all work together around the city, and who knows? We could even have a competition for all the neighborhoods about who has the best or greenest garden. The competition would be just for a fun and good cause—people who would win would receive recognition.

"We could have a competition for all the neighborhoods about who has the best or greenest garden. The competition would be just for a fun and good cause— people who would win would receive recognition."

Jose C.

is fifteen years old. He is from San Diego, California. His first language is Spanish. He likes to play the guitar. He is a lover of soccer and would like to play in a important game. His favorite food is mariscos like ceviche, camaron endiablado, camaron con pulpo, etc. Well, He also loves birria. His favorite brands are Adidas for clothes, and Nike Air for shoes. He likes to write songs and sing and he loves to drive around. He also loves to eat hot chips with chile valentina, while he watches TV.

One Beautiful Day

It all started on one beautiful weekend day; I was at home with my family. They were getting ready to go on a trip to watch baseball. I didn't want to go because I get bored. I think it's a good sport to play but I don't like to watch it for three long hours.

My mom let me stay home alone so there was no problem. When they left, i told some of my friends to come over so we could go to Walmart or a store to get some Flaming Hot Cheetos and something to drink. We went to the park to play soccer. While I was playing, the time went by so fast that, by the time I checked, it was already 7 p.m. I was supposed to be home at 5 p.m. because my family would be back from their trip. I ran home and I was so scared. When I got home, my mom was mad as mad. She punished me and I went to my room all sad. I was thinking crazy things: *instead of being alone in my room, I wish I could teleport to Dubai and be with Shakira at a big party where my friends played soccer with Messi and Neymar Jr., while Shakira sang.*

Chicago Needs Me

Haciendo un Chicago mejor, un Chicago nuevo, un Chicago de felicidad, de alegrías. No hay tristezas, no hay agonías, no hay depresiones, no hay violencia, no hay abuso, no hay pandillas. Un Chicago donde la maldad y el lado negativo no existan.

Quiero un Chicago vivo, un Chicago donde la gente se lleve bien con la gente, un Chicago donde haya muchas culturas diferentes con muchos idiomas diferentes donde la gente comparta y se ría con los demás, que no importe el color, la raza ni las tradiciones. Un Chicago donde haya restaurantes de cada país: mexicano, argentino, español, chino, japonés, de todas las comidas tradicionales de cada raza que hay en el mundo. Este sería mi Chicago realista donde la gente tuviera trabajo y una vida normal, pero habrá otro Chicago. En este mismo Chicago habrá una puerta gigantesca en una esquina llena de flores con letras grandes que dicen "BIENVENIDO A CHICAGO HEAVEN" en cualquier idioma. La gente puede entrar y salir cuando quiera; en ese misterioso Chicago habrá mucha fantasía, mucha magia, y al abrir las puertas verás un lugar hermoso, lleno de casas bonitas donde la gente descansa y convive con los demás debajo de un cielo, donde el agua es su compañera fiel, donde los peces y cualquier animal marino pueden nadar sin lastimar a la gente porque este Chicago no conoce el dolor. Es una selva gigantesca donde hay animales de todo tipo que son libres, que se divierten con la gente, y en ese Chicago Heaven habrá un edificio grande donde hay salones de videojuegos, salones de belleza para mujeres, salones de deportes, salones de música de todo para que la gente vaya y explore su imaginación y se divierta haciendo lo que le gusta o lo que ama hacer. Este Chicago será enorme; siempre será de día. No habrá oscuridad, pero habrá un cuarto donde es de noche, pero las estrellas y luna brillan, un cielo donde se ve todas la galaxias, donde la gente puede ir a observar y pasar tiempo con sus familias y amigos.

En este Chicago la música será de todas las tradiciones, pero será algo como que la canción que la gente escoja será la única que se puede escuchar. Todas las personas tendrán un reloj que les habla, para ser su guía, que les avisa todo lo nuevo que hay en este mundo. En este Chicago sí nevará, pero la temperatura no bajará de los 30* grados, para que la gente pueda jugar y divertirse con la nieve sin pasar fríos.

Arriba, muy arriba de este Chicago, habrá una cápsula que se mantiene arriba. Será un lugar donde se juega a todos los deportes y cada medio año habrá torneos de cada deporte. Será un lugar enorme donde puede entrar toda la gente. Para llegar hacia arriba habrá un trampolín donde la gente brinca y sube hasta arriba y aparece dentro de la cápsula. Y al lado habrá un tubo que absorbe todas las cosas y las pertenencias de la gente para que no tenga que cargarlas. Cuando empiezan los torneos habrá unos de los mejores reporteros que habla en un idioma que todos entienden, que se nombrará "loveit." Toda la gente habla este idioma para que toda la gente disfrute el torneo. Pero todavía falta más: habrá robots que vuelan y caminan ofreciendo de comer a toda la gente nachos, hotdogs, hamburguesas, chips, snacks, etc.

Cuando gana un solo campo o equipo de cada deporte se harán unas estatuas en un parque de cada campeón, para honrarlos con este hermoso premio; cada medio año habrá un campeón y ganador. Y al terminar el torneo habrá una fiesta enorme, tipo "feria," para terminar el día alegre, donde habrá juegos, juegos electrónicos de todo tipo.

Brian F.

is a sixteen-year-old dude. Brian's favorite things to do is to play sports and watch sports. Brian likes baseball, soccer, and boxing. He also likes to play videogames. Brian likes sports videogames and first-person shooter games. He likes Mexican food and Italian food. He hopes that in the future he gets to play in the MLB.

My Chicago

My Chicago would look clean—there's not going to be trash in the streets. My Chicago is going to have all types of food no matter where you're from—there's going to be food from your culture—pizza, tacos, pasta—everything you can think of. My Chicago would be safe, children would be able to run around have fun at a playground without their parents having to worry about anything. Everyone would have free Wi-Fi and we would have the best technology. Everyone in Chicago would have a roof above their heads and food—no one is going to be poor. Every sport would be shown on TV and sports events are going to be in Chicago like soccer, baseball, basketball, any sport would be in my Chicago.

Everyone would respect each other like family, everyone would help each other, and be super friendly. Schools would have cool playgrounds for kids and have everything they need, food would be good—not that nasty frozen stuff, all the bathrooms would be clean and the classrooms would be super clean. There won't be any homework. Houses would be big in my Chicago and no one would live in the streets—everyone would live in a house with everything that a person needs.

"Everyone would respect each other like family."

TAKE A PAGE FROM...

Esmeralda

Take a look at pages 96-97.

Make a comic with at least 8 panels that depicts problems you see in Chicago and your ideas for solutions.

The last panel should be a drawing of your Chicago heaven.

Esmeralda G.
is fifteen years old.
She goes to George
Washington High
School. What she really
likes to do is draw and
do anything that has to
do with art. She likes
anything to do with
plants and animals.
Esmeralda really likes
music and writing her
own. She plays video
games and likes to
read books. She enjoys
working on art projects
for classes. She's very
shy but will open up
when you get to know
her. All she wants is to
have a good career.

Chicago Needs Me...

Chicago needs me and I'm going to
change it by adding more green places.
One way we can add more green in our
city is by adding more forest and parks
so people can enjoy the outdoors and
have fun seeing the animals and birds.
We can also break down old houses or
other buildings that we don't need so we
can add more trees to breathe or, even
better, homes for homeless people.

We could also have an animal
shelter so we can also protect our
amazing animals for the future and
have a chance of lowering the risk of
extinction. For the animal shelter, we
can build a big glass-domed building
were we can have all types of animals
and plants so we can see how they grow
and help them. When we have enough
plants, we can move them to places
where lots of plants have been gone
for years and make our planet better
and stronger. It will also be helpful
for school because we can learn about
animals and plants.

What if we also had homeless people
help and earn money by cleaning our
forests, parks, and even homes? It could
make people want to live in Chicago
and enjoy the outdoors more. They will
know how important it is to take care
of our planet and how we can help our
planet, forests, and animals by doing
something. We can start by making a
city that is known for its greenery and
animals and we can start with Chicago.

Laisha F.

(grade 9) attends
George Washington
High School, is fourteen
years old, and always
wears her hair in a bun.
She absolutely adores
dogs. She is always
in a cheerful mood,
but she doesn't like to
smile a lot. She loves
cheesecake. Her friends
think that she is laid
back. She loves Netflix.
She loves visiting her
cousins and getting to
hang out with them. She
hopes to travel the world
someday with her family
and friends.

My Chicago

Chicago needs me and I'm going
to change it by having more shelters
for people. The shelters will come
with rooms for one to sleep in and a
little kitchen and dining area where
they can eat. It will also come with a
bathroom. It will basically be like a
little apartment so everyone can have
privacy and be comfortable. I also
want for everyone to have a job that
will keep them on their feet. I can
have a job fair where a lot of different
businesses come with information
about the jobs and bring applications
with them so that people can sign up.

I would also like more
gardens. In each park, there could be
a garden that would be supervised
so people won't have to worry about
someone damaging their plants.
Parents can bring their kids to plant a
flower of their choice. They can plant
as many as they would like. They will
be shaped into big rectangles with
materials so that the kids can put
their names, put something that they
like, and something that represents
who they are. In the park there can
be a section where families can bring
their dogs to play in. It will have dog
toys and other things that will consist
of them running, jumping, walking,
etc. Each dog will get a brand new toy
each time that they go.

Jervany C.

is a freshman in Chicago who loves to play basketball. He is working on basketball, mostly his shooting and dribbling. For the most part, his driving skills are on point. He enjoys playing games with his friends, especially Fortnite and 2K. His dislikes include seafood, which is nasty and salty, and golf, which is a very boring sport.

The Game Winner

One day there was a basketball game, and it was a big game for us. If we won, we would go to state. During the game, our best player got hurt. We were winning, but the other team caught up and took the lead by three. We were basically done, but someone got an 'and one' from the three-point line. This free throw determined the game, *so the dude shot it, and the rim opened so wide that when it left his hands, it automatically went in and we won state.*

Karina N.

is a fourteen-year-old girl. She considers herself a born and semi-raised Chicagoan because she spent some time living in Florida. Karina's favorite thing to do is to be happy and make memories with the people she loves. For extracurricular activities, Karina plays soccer; her position is mid- or defense right-back. When she's older, she wants to travel the world and learn about different cultures.

Bettering Chicago For Our Future

Chicago needs me, and I am going to change it by making homes for the homeless, renovating all CPS schools, and cleaning up the city. I chose these three ideas because they affect our city and our youth. We can provide rehabilitation for homeless and get them a job and put them in government housing. We can set up renovations for CPS schools so their students can catch up with the rest of their generation and have everything they may need. Clean ups in Chicago are mandatory because our city suffers with pollution and clean up days should be an obligation.

Homes for the homeless can include many things, not just a home itself. As a city we can provide and make our homeless people working-class citizens with our help. We can help them get off the streets and reduce the percentage of homeless getting killed or raped or into drugs. As a large community we have to remember that even though they may be less fortunate than us, we have to gather as a community to make our city a better place. We can make rehabilitation centers and divide people into the groups that help them with their current situations, for instance, aid for homelessness, having no money, having a drug addiction, experiencing sexual harassment or mental illness. An example of this kind of aid might be that the homeless with no money would join a class to show them how to take care of themselves and help with any of their needs and give them a home and a job to start their new life.

Renovation for all CPS schools may include getting their technology up to date. It also may include adding on to the school or building new ones that have fewer problems. Schools are an important part of our life and we should be able to enjoy them. We can put programs in place that can suit everys student's interests. We should also pay more attention to students with disabilities by creating more accessible bathrooms and comfortable environments and putting more teachers and aids in place who specialize in working with students with special needs. To get students who may not be so involved in school as a community, we can hold fundraisers and school carnivals to show the benefits of school and how much you can learn and be a part of something bigger than yourself. School improvements would include expanding schools and making them bigger to add students from all diverse backgrounds. Classrooms should be smaller so children can have a better chance of learning and getting one-on-one help. Although children are often not excited for school, we'll put different projects in place in every class to keep the children intrigued and ready to go to school. These projects could come from having extracurricular classes or even elective classes that are designed to students' interests and their future careers. Schools are what make our city knowledgeable and we as a community need to make them better to ensure that all of our youth get a great education.

Our city has suffered with pollution for a long time. Our city is a beautiful place, but can be even more beautiful if we help clean up. I believe we should have Clean Up Days every Sunday and pick a select few residents of Chicago to help clean up. We can make it an obligation like jury duty, but the youth participate as well. This can work by having at least one community at a time clean up another community, whether that be a more high-class neighborhood or low-class neighborhood. This would help Chicago to become more diverse as well as do something great in cleaning up neighborhoods. This will look like families from all over Chicago meeting new people in their city and keeping their homes clean. We as a whole need to learn how to love and take care of our city to ensure that in the future our family still has it. Chicago is our home and we need to work as a community to nurture it in any we can.

Joseph S.

is a fourteen-year-old
freshman at George
Washington High
School. Joseph likes
to play basketball and
one time he dunked
on some kid named
Giovanni R. and got
second place.

No Guns In Chicago

I want to take guns out of Chicago
so everybody will feel safer walking
around and nobody will get shot.
Guns kill people. Even if a person is
not being shot at, they can get shot
by accident or on purpose. Guns
should only be for cops. There could
be a machine that goes in someone's
house and checks it for guns. If they
have a gun, the machine will take
it. That will make the city way safer,
but still not completely safe. More
people could walk around with
their friends or family.

I would also like to stop time
and fly so if someone shoots at me
or somebody else, I could stop the
bullet in mid-air. If somebody is
using a different weapon to attack
someone, I could fly to them and
help them. Everybody will be
happier. Only the babies won't have
superpowers. All the teens will have
them and the babies get them when
they turn seventeen.

"I would also like to stop time and fly so if someone shoots at me or somebody else, I could stop the bullet in mid-air."

What would Chicago look like if you/young people were in charge?

You can use this sentence to get you started:

Chicago needs me and I'm going to change it by...

Darron J.

is a fourteen-year-old freshman student at George Washington High School. Darron's favorite place is Six Flags Great America. What he loves most is music or rapping in the middle of his sixth period art class. One thing he dislikes is fake people who like talking about people behind their back.

Chicago, The Dream

I want money for schools and reserved forest for animals.I also want more attractions and buildings and I want the city to have parties every weekend.

The parties are going to have a lot of different things: if you want to go to a Mexican party, just go to the East Side, we got you. If you want a Puerto Rican party, just go to Humboldt Park, we got that, too. If you want to be at a Black party, just go to the South Side or West Side, or even part of Uptown. Downtown, you'll see a lot of white people. You won't hear the same kind of music; you'll hear the different sounds from all cultures.

Lake Shore Drive is where you can hear all of the above, where the city is lit up with different kinds of sounds of music and the parties don't have a specific kind of food. These parties are just about people getting along without worrying about getting judged by others. As long as that happens, we wouldn't have to worry about violence because rival gangs would be hanging out and wouldn't even notice they're rivals until after the party. Then, they'll notice their opps are not as bad as they thought. One thing about gang violence—it's not for fun or somebody wilding, no, it's survival. I would rather have all the gangs come together. There, violence is over. If I make all the races come together and have a good time, they will learn the other races are better than they seem. Racism will fade away and stereotypes will be gone.

TAKE A PAGE FROM...
Darron

"You won't hear the same kind of music; you'll hear the different sounds from all cultures."

What music would you hear throughout your Chicago?

*no one is
a collage of
others,
you just are
who you are.*

Dalia G.

is a freshman in Chicago who enjoys spending time alone but also getting to know those around her. Although she puts in minimal effort in a lot of her work, somehow, her luck gets her far. She loves making people feel loved and included. Dalia enjoys music and likes filling the silence with random humming and singing. Dalia tries her best to be a good friend and is always supportive of her besties.

Organic n Safe

the warmth of the air is comforting and
welcoming,
the heat radiating from the sun.
it's bright and fuzzy.
you can be outside embracing the wind.
mentally photographing the scenery,
it's not man-made it's organic.

by default, everybody can express
themselves.
no one is a collage of others,
you just are who you are.

it's not an emotional rollercoaster to be
where you want to be,
it isn't a ferris wheel where you feel like
you're at the top of the world for just a bit.
chicago is our place,
our safe place.

Gabriel S.

is fifteen years old and is a freshman at George Washington High School. Gabriel is a good kid who loves sports such as basketball, baseball, and football. He grew up and lived on the East Side of Chicago his whole life. His favorite thing to do in his free time is to hang out with his friends and family. In the future, he sees himself in the NBA or NFL, even though those are hard goals. He says, "I just gotta keep my head up high and my dream alive."

The Blocked Shot

Back in 8th grade, I was in a basketball game. It was the fourth quarter. We were down two with four seconds left and we needed a two-pointer to tie and a three-pointer to win. It was a great game and you could feel the energy of everybody in the building. There was a musty type of smell in the gym, but what can I say? We were basketball players. My team and I decided that we were going to go for the win, but when I shot, it got blocked.

All of a sudden, the ball just started to move by itself, and it was going toward the hoop. It was all in slow motion, but after a while, it went in and everybody started cheering, acting like nothing had just happened.

Chicago

Chicago needs me and I am going to change it by making everyone who is poor wealthier—I'm not saying rich—just so they have enough to get around for their life. Chicago is a beautiful city, don't get me wrong, but I think it's starting to get worse day-by-day. For everyone's safety there is going to be a stricter gun license for only the people who don't have a criminal record. I am also going to make sure that Chicago is never cold somehow because it's too cold, so the temperature will always be fifty to ninety degrees and I think that is fair.

One thing I will for sure do is make sure that the Bulls, Bears, Sox, etc. will all win a championship. I say this because all of our teams are kinda struggling besides the Bears and Cubs. The Bulls are doing badly and that's rare. The best players in the world are going to be on each team, so for basketball Lebron and Kevin Durant will be on the Bulls, and the Bears will have Antonio Brown and Tom Brady even though I don't like him. But you get what I'm trying to say: if you come to my Chicago, there will be a guaranteed championship every year.

The food will be the best food ever made—I'm talking about the best of the best. Seafood, Mexican food, you get the point. But every single piece of food in my Chicago will be free so the homeless will be able to eat whenever they want.

Estefani M.

is a freshman at George Washington High School. Estefani is fourteen years old. She loves to sleep and take naps. Estefani loves playing soccer and volleyball; she may not be the best player, but practice makes perfect. Estefani is super excited about her *quinceañera*.

Chicago Needs Me...

Chicago needs me, and I'm going to change it by not having any school so people can just lie around and hang out with friends. And everyone gets $500 in their bank accounts every day so they can pay for food and the phone bill. I also would make it so the people here had NO electricity or gas bills. People ONLY work on Mondays and Tuesdays. Whenever a new phone comes out we will give the first hundred out for free. Free FAST WiFi anywhere you are in case you don't have a cable line. We'll have two days for being active or playing sports in the week. You can still be active other days, but you should have two days from the week that you take at least one hour for being active. Also, you can join college early.

"Everyone gets $500 in their bank accounts every day so they can pay for food and the phone bill. I also would make it so the people here had NO electricity or gas bills. People ONLY work on Mondays and Tuesdays."

TAKE A PAGE FROM...

ADRIAN

> "There would be less school time in Chicago. . . In other countries, kids have less school time and they rank higher than American students."

Are there policies from other countries you would borrow for your new Chicago?

Adrian E.
is a student at George Washington High School.

The Chicago Dream

Chicago needs me and I'm going to change it by lowering taxes and bills for everyone. That way they don't have to worry about money and that way people can do what they want like hang out with friends, go places, and explore the city. Buildings and houses will be rebuilt into bigger and better ones, and for the outside of each, there would be a big yard to run around and you could put cars there or things like a trampoline or whatever you want. And for the inside, there would be a carpet. If you want, there would be a basement and upstairs, and the houses would be wide, too, like they would almost be as wide as the biggest backyard you've ever seen. Trees and grass, too. I will make sure there is no animal cruelty. Food and drinks won't be as expensive as they are today. Also, buildings can be put near Lake Michigan or any other type of water. Anything can be given free to you if you have a good reason for it. Everybody gets paid 30 percent more than their normal paycheck. Streets would be fixed so that everyone can drive safely without worrying about getting into an accident.

In my Chicago, there would be more animals in the zoos of different species so that people and kids could see and study them. No guns would be allowed, not even for police officers, and everybody has a therapist, but it's optional to go to one if you want.

Also there would be less school time in Chicago like in other countries and states, because not every child or teenager likes to go to school and stay there for seven to eight hours. In other countries, kids have less school time and they rank higher than American students. Having American students wake up early for school is just tiring. I think school should start at 8:30 and end by 1:30. That way kids and teenagers can still learn what they have to and not worry about waking up early for school, and so they have more time to hang out with friends and family members. There would be no homework unless you want extra credit for it, so kids can get their grades up when it starts to get low.

Homeless people would have houses and apartments to live in instead of the streets, but only ones that behave and don't do things that are bad or get others harmed. Also I would clean and fix the streets and pay the construction men more if they did it faster instead of taking months, because everybody gotta go somewhere fast but the roads, buildings, and bridges are taking too long to fix.

Luis C.

is a fifteen-year-old who goes to George Washington High School. He likes to go out with friends and hang out. He's super funny and sometimes rude, according to some people. Luis is good at many things including sports and school. One of his many dreams is to become a photographer.

Paradise

Chicago needs me and I'm going to change it by building every person a house and by providing jobs for them. The homeless will get my attention first. Then I'll pay attention to the gun problem. After everyone is stable and able to provide for themselves, we'll move on. I'll give a speech for everyone to just put down the weapons and make peace. It works, so now it's time to address the buildings. We'll add more buildings with a little medieval vibe to them and with beautiful gardens. Everyone will love going outside and socializing. More land will be added to Chicago to build the houses just in case you're wondering where the houses are going to be. Everyone will have a very wonderful time.

"I'll give a speech for everyone to just put down the weapons and make peace. It works…"

TAKE A PAGE FROM...

Graciela

"Schools would look nice inside classrooms, the teachers would have nice desks to do their work on and new boards so they can teach their students. New desk, new floors, new walls, you name it . . ."

What changes would you make to Chicago's schools?

Graciela G.

is fifteen and she's from East Side Chicago. Gracie loves to play soccer and volleyball. She has the loudest laugh and the funniest jokes. She makes a lot of mistakes, but always finds a way to fix them. She is nice to everyone and is positive in every situation. She loves her friends and loves to have fun. Of course, her favorite food is pizza and she loves her niece and nephew. Netflix is her strong suit.

What Would My Chicago Look Like?

First I would want to run my city of Chicago, and it would be amazing. I would want things to change in my city. I would want better communities with people helping and providing for their families and friends. I would like to change the way people live and how they treat people.

In Chicago, there's a lot of violence in a lot of areas. There's a lot of gun violence and a lot of racism around here. I would want more police to be more involved and take action on what's going on in Chicago. Well, I'm not saying I know too much about police officers, but I do know I want to be one someday in the future and make a difference. I want to save people and stop violence in the streets, and in homes.

I would want to fix the schools, because some of the schools are ugly, ruined on the inside and out. Schools would look nice inside classrooms, the teachers would have nice desks to do their work on and new boards so they can teach their students. New desk, new floors, new walls, you name it . . . I want students to be excited walking into the school building and ready to learn. I would want students to be eating healthy food. I want better education for all students. I wouldn't want any student dropping out of school. It really bothers me that kids drop out of school and they have useless jobs that don't provide for their family or not even for themselves. Maybe people can try to like to learn and be well educated. So when they get older, they'll know what to do in life and be ready for the jobs they want.

I would want my Chicago to be full of art and color everywhere. I want the weather to be beautiful in Chicago—hot but not hot all the time. I can't wait for my changes in Chicago.

"I would make a machine that runs on garbage. That machine goes around and picks up trash on the streets and parking lots, throws it into a hole, and powers itself."

Adrian V.

is a fourteen-year-old from Chicago and is a freshman at George Washington High School. Adrian loves to play video games likes Fortnite, NBA 2K19, and GTA 5. He likes to play basketball in his backyard and in the park. He also enjoys going to school and talking to his classmates. Something he wants to do in the future is finish college. The college he would like to go to is the University of Chicago to study Computer Science.

Chicago

Chicago needs me and I'm going to change it by cleaning the streets. When I go out with the family, I always look at the road when we're on our way and see dirty streets, dirty parking lots, and even dirty sidewalks. In my mind I always ask myself, "Why don't people just throw their trash away rather than throwing it on the ground?" It kinda makes me mad, because later on other people are just going to pick it up. I would make a machine that runs on garbage. That machine goes around and picks up trash on the streets and parking lots, throws it into a hole, and powers itself. So, if I made a change in Chicago I would clean the streets.

Another thing is that I would want to stop the shootings. Like yesterday a woman was shot for no reason, and they had the whole area surrounded with police officers. I wouldn't want my Chicago to have shootings. No, I would have everyone love each other and spread positivity. We don't want any more shootings in Chicago now. What if other people around the world wanted to come to Chicago, and once they arrived they heard gunshots. Maybe they wouldn't want to come back, because they might think that it's a dangerous place. So I wouldn't want that in my Chicago.

Like I said earlier, I want everyone to love each other and respect each other and spread positive vibes. We can try to change the minds of people who aren't respecting others by explaining all the good things can happen. We can try and show them how to respect others and how to help the city and others.

One more thing is helping the homeless. Every time I see a homeless person I give them a couple bucks. I don't like it when other people just mistreat the homeless like they don't have lives. In my Chicago, I want to help the homeless by giving them good food. I'm talking like Big Macs, chicken nuggets, burritos, slushies, chicken wings, and more. I would also have them in a place where it's warm and has comfy pillows and soft blankets. This is what I would have in my Chicago!

Juan J.

is fourteen years old.
He attends George
Washington High
School. Juan's favorite
place is California.
What Juan really loves
to do is wrestle. He is
actually really good at
wrestling. Juan is also
a gamer. One thing he
really loves is his family.

Crazy Night

One time I was with friends
and my brother at a skating rink.
My brother is already mean when
he is alone with me. He was being
really mean around our friends.
My brother was acting hard.

I really love my brother, but he
is huge and mean. My brother
is 6-foot-3 and 210 pounds. I
am 106 pounds so he is like a
monster to me. He is like a sea
creature. He looks like shrek. He
dents the earth with his feet. My
friends stick up for my brother if
I tell my mom something he did
to me. I can't tell on my brother.
He never gets in trouble. He is
just a super big blob.

*The rest of the night was fun. I
ignored him. I felt as if I was on water
because the lights reflected from the
ground to my face. I ate candy that
made me feel unstoppable. I was flash
on the rink. I wasn't even getting tired.
I was going so fast I was flying for short
periods of time. I was able to touch the
ceiling. My dreams were coming true. I
put my brother in a princess dress. My
friends were laughing at him. I even
cracked a laugh.*

*Everything was in my powers. I
could be better than others. I finally
controlled my brother. I could get all
the revenge. I thought, why get revenge
that only made me less of a person?*

Young Chicago

Young people controlling Chicago—that's crazy. I am here to explain how Chicago would be if young people controlled Chicago. I think it would be a good, weird, *Zootopia* Chicago.

I am young and I would love to have an opinion in helping to control Chicago. My Chicago would have middle-class people—not any poor people. This will be good for Chicago because no one will ever suffer for money. I would make Chicago a place where there is no death by violence but death by health issues so my Chicago wouldn't overload. Chicago would be so big that everyone will have enough space to live. There would be mountains and free land so everyone and their family can live well. Everyone will be at peace because there will be no worrying about getting killed. Chicago would have no guns or drugs—only healthy drugs.

My Chicago will have many animals that are healthy. There would be people who really care about their Chicago. There wouldn't be trash everywhere. Chicago will always be over sixty-five degrees outside. The beach water would be clear of any bacteria, and there would be no sharks, because sharks are kinda scary. The last and final touch to my perfect Chicago would be a nice skyline and nice buildings all around us.

Chicago would be controlled by a different variety of young people. It would all depend on the person to control Chicago. For example, if it was someone who hangs around bad people with bad vibes, most likely Chicago would be worse than it currently is now. A young teen or non-teen who has a good imagination and is not hanging around bad people would probably make Chicago great and like Zootopia.

Young people also have different mindsets at different ages. Young people have many different hobbies that would be added to our Chicago. Sports, education, and many more varieties will be added to our city. Honestly, I don't think any young person would make Chicago any worse than it is, considering it is pretty bad already.

Jesus F.

(Grade 9) is a fourteen-year-old who attends George Washington High School. Jesus has had diabetes for seven years; he got the illness when he was only eight years old. Jesus loves to read comics and loves to watch Marvel and DC movies (comic nerd). Jesus loves to blast music with his Apple headphones. He says it's just the "vibes that make me, me ". Jesus is just another kid from a bad past who still fights to this day to see the good days. He knows the end will be worth it. Jesus wants to move back to his home in California and find a good paying job out there.

Something I Always Wanted To Re-Do

Something I always wanted to re-do was to listen to my mother when she would tell me who my real friends are. My mother was always right, but being dumb and not listening, I let those "friends" get to me.

Then—boom—a unicorn came outta nowhere and took those friends away. Then I got a cool sword that's so sharp that even by looking at it, you get cut. Not only did the unicorn give me a sword, I also got the gift to think of something and make it come true at the blink of an eye. The unicorn wasn't just any type of unicorn—it also was the rarest one of them all. Only the true chosen one can see it...

Perfect Chicago

When we think of the "Perfect Chicago" and we all think about everything that we want in the city, us "young kids" have a very big mind. As a "youngin" thinking about the city I want, I think of a couple things.

My first creation would be to build homes for those people who don't have a roof over their heads, so they can keep warm and have something called "my home". Many people that I have known didn't and still don't have a home, so giving them something small would make them happy which will later turn into positive vibes for my city.

I always wanted to go out and add more landmarks to downtown because it would just be a great visit and you could take pictures to always remember the fun you had. Whenever I have the time to go visit a landmark, I see the smiles and joy in people's faces and you just can feel those nice vibes. Some of the landmarks would be free but they would be probably twice as big and better. If you believe enough, you can make the landmarks come alive or even move different places.

Chicago Needs Me

Giovanni R.

is a fifteen-year-old freshman at George Washington High School. He likes playing soccer on the weekends. One thing he hates is people who chew with their mouth open. He likes to eat salads. When he grows up, he wants to play professional soccer.

Chicago needs me and I'm going to change it by fixing up schools and increasing security in them in case anything bad happens. When I fix up schools, they're going to be spacious and have big classrooms, nice bathrooms, and the teachers are going to be paid a lot of money. There are going to be at least four floors, but the buildings will be very wide. I also want schools to serve good lunch like tacos, good pizza, and tamales, and instead of milk I'll give everyone water or juice.

Also, in my perfect Chicago, I don't want poverty. All the homeless people will get houses or I'll make buildings for homeless people to walk in and stay. The place where they're going to stay will have different bedrooms and be fancy and big so they can each have space. Also they will be served food whenever they want and given all new clothes.

In my perfect Chicago, I want it to always be summer because it's such a nice city, and if you walk around, you can see more of it. If it's cold, who would want to go out and just be cold? If it's summer I can always be at the beach instead of waking up in the morning to see if it's going to be cold or not. Also, I can go out without a big jacket. I can go out in shorts and the ice cream trucks will always be on my block.

TAKE A PAGE FROM...

Giovanni

"In my perfect Chicago, I want it to always be summer because it's such a nice city, and if you walk around, you can see more of it."

What is the weather in your perfect Chicago? Is it summer? Spring? Winter??

"...Many look down on Chicago for all its violence and don't actually see the good in Chicago and miss how many others love living here, knowing it's their city."

Julissa M.

is a fourteen-year-old freshman at George Washington High School. Julissa's favorite thing is to listen to all types of music. Music is like a therapy to her; it makes her calm and helps her think. She loves listening to a lot of 80/90's hip hop & rap like Tupac, The Notorious B.I.G, and Snoop Dogg. When she grows up she would love to work as a lawyer. She always found cases so soothing and would love to be part of figuring one out. She's a very funny, outgoing, and very loud person. She likes to make other people laugh and that makes her very happy and motivates her a lot. She can be very supportive in many things and that's why many people love her.

Chicago Heaven

Chicago needs me and I'm going to change it by having less hate and more equality, and by being able to change society in a better way. Many people believe in the wrong things and don't think about certain options they have, and they use violence as an answer. A lot of hatred is in the world and society makes us think a lot of stuff.

Another thing I would love to change is homelessness. Everyone is going to have a home. A lot of people suffer in the streets trying to find a home or shelter, and they suffer through a lot like starvation, getting really sick, and having no warmth during the hard seasons. I want to be able to clean up the streets to have a better environment and less gang violence. Having more green—plants and better. I want to find a shelter for all the animals in the street and for all the endangered animals to be safe again, so we don't worry about them going away.

This Chicago heaven will have a different look, because many look down on Chicago for all its violence and don't actually see the good in Chicago and miss how many others love living here, knowing it's their city.

James P.

is fourteen years old. He is funny because he loves to tell jokes. This teenager is smart, because he enjoys learning a lot. He is so creative because he makes stuff. He is someone's son and someone's friend. He loves to eat burritos, practice wrestling, and by all means, he loves setting future goals. He will be a graduate, an incredible firefighter, and of course, an amazing human being. This is James.

Chicago Needs Me

Chicago needs me and I'm going to change it by keeping areas safe from danger, because people get hurt. And I'd make the hospitals better, make the medicine better for the people around the city who are ill or have a disease, like cancer. In Chicago schools there's gonna be security cameras and alarms. If there's a tornado or missile strike, there's gonna be a bunker with supplies like food, medicine, and water. The streets will be safe at night because there's gonna be street lights.

Make 3 columns on a piece of paper.

What are some issues in Chicago?	What does Chicago need?	What are some solutions for columns 1 and 2?

Janessa A.

is a fourteen-year-old adolescent and she goes to George Washington High School. Janessa's favorite sport is volleyball. Her favorite food is hot wings. She hates onions and never has them in any of her food so please don't bring them near her because she will have a fit. She has always wanted to go to Paris and Dubai. In the future, Janessa wants to become a physical therapist or be a photographer.

At Practice

One day I was at practice and my coach was trying to teach me how to jump-serve. On the first try I couldn't do it, but I just kept trying until I got it. I didn't think I would get it because I felt so weak. Also, I felt like I looked so goofy when I would jump. When I kept trying, I finally got it, and I was so proud of myself *that I had all the money in the world.* Everyone congratulated me but it really wasn't that big of a deal *because I can just fly my way up to the ball.* Now I'm very consistent with all of my jump-serves and I can do it whenever *I get a new sports car and speed race on the rainbow roads. I feel like I jump really high when I actually try and it works because I can fly and i'm the richest person in the world.*

My Chicago

Chicago needs me and I'm going to change it by having more green everywhere and positive people. Everyone can have fun and live their own life with their own decisions. My Chicago is full of hardworking people, and there are no homeless people or violence. Fun is the definition of my Chicago because everyone is partying all day, every day, and there's never a dull moment. There will always be music playing and people dancing so everyone is always in a good mood and has a good, fun vibe. The parties always have a lot of people in them and everyone is dancing, eating, playing games like cards, etc. People are giving each other compliments all the time, and everyone always has this big, bright smile with some kind of good reason behind it because everyone will have their own happiness.

People are always so happy because they love to live life and go on adventures like going on hikes, walking in the woods, etc. There are animals in all the forests like elephants, giraffes, monkeys, etc. All the days are sunny and bright with blue skies and it never rains or snows. People go to the beach with friends and family, listen to music, dance, eat whatever they want, and just have a good time. Sometimes people even go visit nature and there are wooden houses that anyone can visit with hammocks so they can lay down and relax. There is always a fair open 24/7 so anyone can go and ride roller coasters and have even more fun. There is also a special beach for when you want to go and relax by the water. There are hammocks above the water so you can sit in the sun, and listen and watch the waves below you. You don't even have to wear sunscreen because there is no such thing as a sunburn, you just get a tan if you're out in the sun.

Everyone is rich and there are no more poor people so nobody has to work if they don't want to because it's stressful. There will be robots to do our jobs at stores. You'll see them at cash registers, coffee shops where they will pour your coffee, restaurants where they will be your waitress, etc.

Whenever someone is about to get in a car accident, the car will turn into this gummy-like substance and the cars will bump like bumper cars and no one will ever get hurt. In my Chicago, if someone shoots a gun, gummy bears or whatever your favorite candy is will come out like confetti. No one will get hurt in my Chicago. No one will get physically, mentally, or emotionally hurt.

Janeth M.

is seventeen years old and lives in Chicago. Janeth likes to help others and is a very good person. She likes to have everything ready, in order, and controlled. She loves Mexican food. Janeth has two amazing dogs who she loves so much and her favorite color is blue. Hopefully, Janeth will be a nurse in the future.

Chicago Needs Me

Chicago needs me and I'm going to change it by a making it a good environment—a good place for all the people and animals we see and have.

My Chicago is going to be different from all the cities of United States. It will be fair and it is going to protect every single Chicagoan—I don't care if is a animal or an unborn baby. Yeah, my Chicago is going to be the best city the United States has.

I have the view of this new Chicago: It's going to have more parks and especially one for all dogs who are lost or alone on the street. It's going to have food and water and beds for dogs. It's going to be a refuge for all the dogs.

My Chicago will not allow abandonment of seniors in retirement homes and will not allow abuse of any person. We will help people on the streets find a job, home, and education.

In Chicago it would be good to make a big change about the violence. Violence is a reality but power is more—and we need more change; we need clean streets and we need more police and more education about cases.

Chicago doesn't just want people, it wants dreamers. Now, students continue with a career just for money, and don't go to a good university. Everyone is going to study for a career in my Chicago, Illinois.

My Chicago doesn't accept "no" for an answer. If it is good, it will have a good effect in a situation like a good environment. In Chicago, change is good. You don't have to be scared of the word *no*.

Chicago is mine and yours.
Chicago doesn't have to be scared of change. Chicago wants change.
My Chicago—it's good for you, your family, and for me.

"Chicago doesn't have to be scared of change.

Chicago wants change."

Esmeralda G.

is fifteen-year-old freshmen in Chicago, Illinois. She likes to write and sing her heart out. She dislikes people who think that they're better than others. Esmeralda loves to help those around her who are struggling with something. She wishes to become a photographer or a translator to help those who don't speak English.

A Dream Come True

It was a little after 4:00 p.m., and I was walking home from the bus stop. I took my time so that I wouldn't slip and fall on the ice that littered the ground. As I was walking, I took in my surroundings; all the construction trucks moving back and forth, fixing the streets as they moved, cement trucks pouring cement into the ground. I walked past them and continued my walk home.

I finally arrived home—somehow I managed not to fall. I took off my shoes and made my way to my room. I changed into my pj's and went back downstairs. A couple hours had passed and I was starting to get sleepy, and they were still doing construction outside. I tried to sleep—I tossed and turned but nothing would take away from the sound of them fixing the roads. I put in my headphones, blasted a song and drifted into a deep slumber.

I woke up from my sleep to hear the construction workers still fixing the roads. I sighed in frustration, closed my eyes and wished they would just stop. My eyes went wide from the silence that surrounded me. I jumped up from my position as fast as I could and ran for the door. I sprinted out of my house only to be met with empty streets. I was beyond confused. I took notice of the unfinished streets—how there were still holes in the ground. I closed my eyes and wished the streets to be finished and freshly painted. I opened my eyes back up—my lips curled up into the biggest smile I could make. The streets were nicely done, the paint was neatly added and could be seen.

I was beyond happy. I walked up and down the streets admiring what I did. That's when I realized that the streets still had ice. I decided to do something about it, so I did. I closed my eyes for the last time and I wished for the ice to melt away. I opened my eyes and the sight in front of me blew me away. The ice had melted away and the sun can finally be seen past all of the clouds that once filled the sky. I took my time getting home. As I made my way to my front door I smiled a small smile, remembering what I accomplished. With that final thought, I walked into my house and I made my way to my room where I dreamed about how I changed the streets of where I live.

My Chicago

Chicago needs me and this is how I'm going to change it. First, I'm going to clean all the streets so that they're litter free, then add more security cameras on every street corner and alley. I will also give food and shelter to those who need it, remove the dirt and grime that's covered our lake, and make sure you'll meet the friendliest people you'd ever met.

Imagine walking down the streets of Chicago, needing to watch where you step so that you don't get your shoes dirty with garbage and waste that people have thrown on the ground as they walked. Now imagine walking down the streets of Chicago, not having to worry about getting your shoes dirty of waste. Which would you like? Also, would a clean, polished street look more appealing then a dirty, grimy street that looks like a dump for waste. I think not.

I don't want anyone in my Chicago to feel like they're not safe. I want my Chicago to be the safest place in the world. That's why I'm going to add more cameras on streets. I also want to add more laws for certain things like guns, for example. People shouldn't sleep hoping that they'll see the sun one last time before they leave. They should sleep knowing that they'll see the sun because they will wake up and live to see another day. I'll have people petition for more cameras around the city. Everyone should feel safe, not threatened.

At almost every street corner people are begging for money, saying they don't have a shelter, don't have food. I want to change that. I want to build buildings for them to live in, give them food so that they don't starve—I want them to know that they're safe. I'll give them a new life, a better life.

I want to have a lake that's clean. The lake should be the most beautiful thing to look at, not something you should look away from. Crystal clear water, not disgusting, greenish water. We deserve a lake that we never want to look away from in a good way, not bad.

It seems like everyone now is on their phones. No one really communicates with each other. I don't want that for my Chicago. I want people to greet each other when they walk down the streets. I want people to get to know one another, make new friends. We can't just ignore one another.

That's what I want for my Chicago. I want a place that I admire, that I feel safe in. A place where I can go and help people.

Once I Got Into An Argument

Oscar T.
is a student at George Washington High School.

Once I got into an argument with a teacher. I was with my friends chilling inside the hallways of Jane Addams—I just learned a new soccer trick called "the rainbow," and I wanted to show my friends. I got my friend's pencil pouch, put it between my feet, and—boom—I sent it into the air. As soon as it hit the floor, I heard, "Ayyyyee!!!!" A teacher who was a solid four feet away from the pouch accused me of kicking the pouch at her. She took me straight to the principal's office.

After that a dragon flew into the room, spitting fire, roaring. The teacher and principle got scared and ran out the room. I hopped on my dragon and flew to my house, where I ate and went to sleep. That next morning, I went to school and no one believed me about what had happened. Turns out no one believed the principal either.

What Could Chicago Look Like?

Chicago needs me and I'm going to change it starting with the educational system. Schools will have more funding and there will be stricter requirements to be a teacher such as: you need to have at least two kids and you must live in the area. The students will also judge the quality of teachers. Teachers must be more than just a teacher, they need to be the students' friend.

All the potholes in the entire city will be fixed, with quality, super strong asphalt. I will add drains on every corner. All abandoned buildings will be rebuilt. There will be cameras on every street corner and ten thousand new police officers will be added in every ward. All bridges will be fixed and in operating condition.

"A society without guns would look almost perfect."

Anthony B.

is a fourteen-year-old adolescent. Anthony's favorite place to go to is Six Flags Great America. What he likes about life is that you can do whatever you want but with responsibility. What he dislikes about life is there is too many rules. Anthony loves basketball with a passion and he also helps out his family whenever he can. Anthony is a very smart boy and he also is a athletic person. He knows how to say the alphabet backwards. When he grows up, he wants to be a dentist or eye doctor.

A Push for Gun Control

Chicago needs me and I'm going to change it by fixing gun violence because Chicago is a very bad place when it comes to gun violence. I think we should take away all gun licenses unless you are a police officer or in security. Not only that, but all gun crimes should have a minimum punishment of a year in prison.

We should also have people stop using guns when they are not really necessary. The circumstances are: only use a gun if you see someone doing something bad with, let's say, a knife and you need to help them. If they try to or they do kill someone, the gun may be shot, or if someone is trying to kill you, it may be used, or if they are trying to hurt you, then you may not use it but you will be able to scare them with it. I would make sure that every house has been secured and make sure that the people inside don't have guns unless we have proof that they are security or police. A society without guns would look almost perfect. There would be so much less crime.

Meleni A.

is fourteen years old.
She attends George
Washington High School.
Meleni is a very big fan
of Bad Bunny. Meleni's
favorite dessert to have
is ice cream. Last but
not least, Meleni loves to
play with makeup. One
place Meleni would like
to travel to is Paris; she
has always dreamed of
having a family portrait
next to the Eiffel Tower.

Chicago Needs Me

Chicago needs me and I'm
going to change it by making it
safer, more colorful with more
water around it, and making
it more fun to be around. I'm
going to achieve this by giving
everyone a bodyguard and
putting more lights on the
streets. Everyone that has a
backyard would have a pond
with animals to take care of, or
they will just be around your
backyard to make a good life
change to your life and theirs.

I'm also going to put more
lakes and beaches around the
city for people to come and be
around, and I'll plant flowers
like roses and sunflowers all
around to make it more colorful.
Also, I would like to keep adding
more buildings around the city.

TAKE A PAGE FROM...

MELENI

> "I'm also going to put more lakes and beaches around the city for people to come and be around, and I'll plant flowers like roses and sunflowers..."

What natural elements would you add or take away from your perfect Chicago?

Angel V.

is a fifteen-year-old
freshman. Angel's favorite
place is Mexico. Angel likes
meeting people. He also
likes learning new skills
and loves working hard and
making money. He loves
playing sports and other
cool stuff. He is funny, cool,
and beautiful, unlike other
people. His dream in life is
to make a lot of money and
it doesn't matter how.

I Was Thirteen Years Old

I was thirteen years old
and on my way to school with
my mom, my sister, and my
brother in the car. As we were
on the freeway, we were so
close to crashing into another
man's car, and as soon as that
happened he yelled out "F***
YOU" while he stuck up the
middle finger.

*Right when that happened I
thought to myself, what would
happen if someone just threw
eggs at this man's car for what he
did? The most unexpected thing
happened—it started raining
eggs on his car and his face was
so confused and surprised at the
same time, and I knew he got what
he deserved.*

Chicago Needs Me

Chicago needs me and I'm going to change it by making the streets and people feel safer. Everyone will feel safe walking around and feel free because it will be less crowded. To do this, there needs to be more land so people will feel more free to walk around and so Chicago will look more beautiful. We could keep people safe by reducing crime. Also, we could expand Chicago so we could fit all this stuff together. We could make it safer by enforcing better and safer laws. Chicago also needs more rap and hip hop artists so the city can sound nice too.

Rodolfo S.

is seventeen years old. Rodolfo's favorite place is a soccer field because that is where he forgets everything. He likes to have adventures with his friends, to discover new things, and to have fun with the people who talk to him. What he likes to do more is to get new things so he can show them to the people who don't know. A lot of people like him because he is a nice boy and he likes to help a lot of people. His dream is to have a career as a automotive architect so he can make his father proud.

Our Young Chicago

If I was in charge of Chicago, I would have some nice streets, because in some parts of the city, we have some holes in the middle of the street, and that is a big problem for the people who drive all day. These holes can break your car down or break something important in your tire, and you can cause an accident or some other bad thing can happen. When I get the streets nice, another thing that I will do is that all the people will have super cars. But there is going to be a speed limit for the people who have super cars, because the people who have these cars will get happy and drive fast. The police are going to have super cars because you never know what the people will do.

Another thing that I will like to have in my Chicago is more big buildings so the city can get more tourists. The city will get more money to repair the parts that are ugly. The people are going to be safe because there will be more police in the streets and the police will stop the violence and all the killing that happens in our Chicago. When the people come to our Chicago, they get scared because they think that something is going to happen to them.

One of my big ideas for our young Chicago is that we are going to have very famous stores like Gucci on every corner or every suburb so the people have more access. The people are going to love this because they will look nice. Another thing is that people my age like to drive around with their friends, but sometimes they get in an accident because of the insecurity or because the streets are very ugly. I want to have the best Chicago for everyone so we can live with great generations, but at the same time, it's going to be hard for all the killing that is happening here.

If we add police stations, I think we can solve big problems because I want to have the best city for everyone and for me. The thing that I like to do in my free time is drive around because I can clear my mind and forget every problem that I have. I know there are a lot of people who like to do the same thing, and they tell me the streets are ugly no matter where they go.

"I want to have the best Chicago for everyone."

Karla A.
is a student at George Washington High School.

Chicago me necesita y voy a cambiarlo...

por tener una mejor vida, poder poner una mejor seguridad para que las personas se sientan cómoda entre si, poder bajar el numero de la delincuencia. Que en teoría ayudará a la policía a combatir la violencia generada por ajustes de cuentas entre pandillas. Policía justifica el uso del algoritmo al indicar que le permitirá enfocarse en personas que tengan más tendencia a cometer actos con armas de fuego, o a sufrir los.

Jazmine L.

is fourteen years old and in ninth grade at George Washington High School. Jazmine loves dancing; she is a pro. She loves to express her feelings by painting. It's not her passion but it helps her know how she's feeling. She loves being on her phone. It is like part of her life, not in a weird way though. Her dream is to become a entrepreneur and to train horses.

Chicago Seasons

Chicago needs me and I'm going to change it by making things safer and adding bright, vibrant colors everywhere. There would be different types of flowers: lavender, amaryllis, etc. In my Chicago, every step you take, more and more flowers grow and more and more keep appearing. It's peaceful and calming. Just smelling the lavender in the air will make you feel relaxed. Every time someone does something good, more and more flowers grow.

Walking downtown, the weather is changing and turning into spring. There are fewer flowers, it's getting a little less warm, and it's cloudier. It looks like it's going to rain. The sunlight is not as bright as summer and every time you do something bad, lightning bursts out of the clouds. People are walking toward summer and you're just exploring and going the opposite way. You're walking but noticing that you're getting more and more tired.

You put your hand down and you wait for a rainbow taxi to pick you up to take you to fall. You start to see that leaves are on the ground and falling off the trees and the taxi gets to the sidewalk. The driver tells you, "Welcome to Fall. Have a nice time and cover up, it's a little colder here. Avoid trying the hot chocolate. They just want to bring you back to where you started and you really don't want to start all over again."

TAKE A PAGE FROM...

Maleena

"I think anger is a big part of violence. . ."

Are we doing enough to address factors that lead to violence?

If not, what can we do now and in the future?

Maleena G.
is a student at George
Washington High School.

A New Plan

Chicago needs me and I'm going to change it by starting to make more notice of the violence in our city. In order to do this, I would take away all guns, I would encourage people to use stress relievers, or I would have a building full with sports clubs you can join so that you can relieve anger. I think anger is a big part of violence because when people get upset, they automatically get a rush inside to do something without thinking about the consequences of their actions. This way there will be reduced violence in Chicago.

Lizvette M.

(fourteen) is a freshman who attends George Washington High School in Chicago. Lizvette likes to play around a lot but knows when to be serious. She loves spending time with her friends and family and loves to play soccer. She also likes to binge-watch shows on Netflix. She likes to help out people who are in need and tries to be there for people when they need her.

My Chicago

Chicago needs me and I'm going to change it by making it safer and cleaner. I'm going to make it safer because there are lots of traumatic things going on in the world right now, and we need to make our environment safer. Safe means not being afraid to walk the streets in daylight or even at night. We should not be afraid of walking home alone, but with all these terrible things happening, we are scared of our every move. I'm going to make Chicago cleaner because there is a lot of pollution right now, and there is so much garbage everywhere. It is not sanitary.

I'm also going to change Chicago by adding more cultural food restaurants. For example, more Chinese restaurants, more Thai food restaurants, more Indian food restaurants, etc. Things like that for everyone to enjoy. I would also put in more cultural places downtown for everyone to visit so they can experience some of the things other cultures do. For example, downtown has a place called Chinatown, and people love going there because they get to see different things and Chinese culture. It's something different to enjoy. I would also put in more fashion clothes, but at low prices. Right now Gucci, Michael Kors, Champion, Nike, Adidas, North Face, Calvin Klein, etc. are very popular but very expensive. I would like to put more stores like that in locally and at lower prices. I would also put in new rides for the festivals that go on every summer. People all over town love going to the festivals that are planned in the summer and they loving going with their friends and family. Mostly everybody goes for the rides, but since these rides have been here for many years, most of them are very old and are breaking down, which isn't good. I want to put in rides that no one has quite experienced and rides that people would actually get on and have fun.

All these ideas are stuff that I would like to see in my Chicago and that I think other people would like to see. Something that all of these have in common is that they are all in Chicago, and they are all things to make my Chicago a better place. I think we should have a calm, clean, and worthy type of Chicago.

"Safe means not being afraid to walk the streets in daylight or even at night. We should not be afraid of walking home alone..."

"Immigrants will have more opportunities; they can study and have their dream job, and they can express themselves in this city and feel proud of themselves and their city."

Victor S.

is a sixteen, almost-seventeen-year-old. Victor's favorite place is a restaurant called Uncle Julio's. He is noble and he treats you nicely if you treat him nicely. He likes nice things. Maybe in his life, he might finish college so he can be an architect and help his family. Victor likes things that are challenging because he can improve his work and become capable. He likes to go to the movies and practice soccer and boxing.

Everyone is Equal

Chicago needs me and I'm going to change it by giving a new life to poor people. I'm going to try to pull them out of drugs and make sure they are working and not doing bad stuff. I will give an apartment to those who are poor and not doing drugs and also to the ones who did drugs, but I will make sure that they are cured and not going to do drugs again.

I will try to decrease the violence—I know violence is never going to stop, but we can decrease it and make neighborhoods safer. To decrease the violence, I might add police to patrol the city almost all the time and at night. The police will search for criminals and see if the cars on the street look suspicious—they will check backgrounds of everyone who has criminal records. I will give them the best technology so operations can go better than we planned.

I will call for more art so artistic people can be be more inspired and more successful. I will add more museums of history and of the new things that are happening around the world. I will add more churches for people who are religious and try to add a lot of space in these churches. In Chicago, we have a lot of religious people, and this would benefit Chicago because the churches are for people to pray in, and they would know about the history of the churches. I will add more buildings, but I'm also going to try to save the planet from pollution and grow more trees. I will fix all the schools with more books and technology, and I'll make them safer with more police and security.

I will make all communities the same—everyone is equal—no one is better than the other. I will give a better life to everyone—even the poor people. I'm going to make healthcare better for everyone. There is going to be more work—even for immigrants, and there will be more protection in the streets. Immigrants will have more opportunities; they can study and have their dream job, and they can express themselves in this city and feel proud of themselves and their city. I would put more protection in the streets: I will put more officers going around neighborhoods and officers with dogs—if they detect something wrong, they can help. I will call for the building of more police stations on every corner of the city. I might put more restaurants so people can work and have more money. I might make taxes lower so we pay less taxes.

Write 20 lines that all start with the phrase "I dream."

Think about what you dream of, what you wish you could say or do, where you wish you could really be.

I dream...   I dream...

I dream...   I dream...

I dream...   I dream...

I dream...   I dream...

I dream....   I dream...

I dream...   *I dream...*

I dream...   *I dream...*

I dream...   *I dream...*

I dream...   *I dream...*

I dream...   *I dream...*

Let your mind go anywhere silly or nonsensical.

Write for 5 minutes- try to write quickly, when you feel yourself getting stuck, just keep on going, do not let the pen stop touching the paper.

Jose G.

is a student at George Washington High School.

How I Want You to Look at Chicago

If I could change things in the city of Chicago, the main thing I would change would be all the police and the authorities that are responsible for the safety of the people. I would do that for the simple reason that there are police officers who are influenced by corruption because there are too many police officers who unexpectedly find drugs and all kinds of illegal substances. To be more specific, on the subject of corrupt authorities, every so often the boss would change the officers' routes and put cameras inside the patrol cars to observe what each of them does.

Also I would raise all salaries because there are many people who work for a salary that is not enough to support a family, even though their jobs are very tiring and they work too many hours. Despite that, they earn a very low amount.

I would hire people to clean every park, street or any place that looks very dirty in the city. Of course those people would have a very high salary.

I would add more homeless shelters for people who really need help, such as senior citizens who live on the streets and do not have enough strength to get a job. I would also start campaigns for people with severe illnesses like cancer. In those campaigns, they would get help financially with necessary medications and free consultations. I would create more opportunities for young people with a future in soccer by helping them with school and with soccer so that little by little they will improve so they can get on a good team and excel.

I would increase opportunities for young people who want to go to college. I will help them financially or offer them scholarships for their performance in college so that they can achieve their goals.

TAKE A PAGE FROM...

Jose

> "I would add more homeless shelters for people who really need help, such as senior citizens who live on the streets and do not have enough strength to get a job."

What overlooked populations would you try to help in your Chicago heaven?

Fernando S.

is a fifteen-year-old
freshman at George
Washington High School.
Fernando likes to play
soccer. Fernando also likes
to watch soccer. Fernando
dislikes rudeness in people
as it is annoying. Fernando
likes to help out his family
and he likes the sense of
having unity inside his
family. His dreams are
to become a professional
soccer player and be rich.

Once I Was Walking Down The Street

Once I was walking down
the street. It was a sunny day.
The birds were chirping. I was
thinking while watching the
blue skies. I was so caught up
in my thoughts that I fell. I got
up and it hurt a little, but I got
through it. Then, I saw another
person also looking up at the
sky and they also fell. I turned
around and giggled.

*Then a genie popped up and
stopped time. He asked me to give
him three wishes. I asked for an
unlimited amount of wishes. Then
I asked for neither of us to trip.
I wished I was immortal and a
professional soccer player. I went on
to live a rich, immortal life.*

Posi-Cago

Chicago needs me and I'm going to change it by making sure everyone is able to walk around their neighborhood and not have worries on their mind. Everyone will be walking down the sunny streets with other people who have smiles on their faces. No one is in a rush and no one is having a bad day. People are stopping to talk to each other. People are caring, not selfish. When someone's groceries fall or they fall, people will help. Everyone can walk around knowing that there is no harm. There are no more sick-minded people. Racism isn't a thing in my Chicago; everyone has respect for each other. No one is above anyone. There is equality. Everyone enjoys each other's culture. If a man is wearing a sombrero, there would be a story behind it that would be told.

Everyone is enjoying their best life. No judgement. If someone out of town comes to the new Chicago and they're completely different, people won't stare and act awkward or laugh at their differences. They would admire them. People would come together as a community to unite as one to help all the people that have bad past experiences not be in that bad-minded stage. Chicago looks ten times more beautiful. The reconstruction of Chicago began and all the positivity led to faster work. Everyone had a say in what we should add. The constructive criticism led to everything being nicer.

Yemilette L.

is fifteen years old and is a freshman. She attends George Washington High School. She plays volleyball and soccer. She has been in Chicago since day one. She enjoys going out with her friends and doing fun things. She loves eating chips. She also is a really nice person and funny sometimes. She likes doing her makeup all the time.

CHICAGO!!!!

Chicago needs me and I'm going to change it by making it more beautiful than it is already. I'll make more exciting things like activities and clubs that kids would be interested in and would want to be there often. Bright, shining stuff. Making the city a little different.

I also want to follow my dreams and do what I want. I want to make some of my dreams come true. Not all of them of course—I mean I think it is possible, but I'll be happy with only at least three of them. There are at least a few people who would want to change something about Chicago. People have different opinions about different things that they don't like. Like me—when I grow up, I want to be a nurse. Maybe later on in life I'll change my mind.

After graduating from high school, you don't have to stop—you still need college in order for you to have a good job and get better money. You want the best for your kids and you want them to have all you can give them. What I want Chicago to know is that everyone could do good. Not everyone is perfect. Anyone could make any mistakes. Chicago has some things that are not perfect either. Keep your grind going—don't give up. Everybody has a second chance or many more chances—if you give up, you could still try again later on or at that same time. There will always be a spot for anybody no matter what, or they'll look for a spot for you. Never give up. Everyone wants money, but you have to work hard to earn it. For example, if you want a car you have to earn money to save up so you can buy it yourself. It's hard—it's not easy once you grow up. We can all make a huge difference. We just have to work together to come up with ideas.

"We can all make a huge difference. We just have to work together to come up with ideas."

Mia M.

is fifteen years old and attends George Washington High School. Mia likes to play volleyball and softball to keep her busy throughout the season. She loves to go out and have some fun with her friends and family. In her view, Mexican food is the best food out there, especially tacos/tortas. Mia enjoys watching romantic comedies and horror movies. Mia also enjoys doing makeup for a living and wants to do makeup when she is older.

Homecoming Chaos

A time I wish I could've acted differently was with a boy. I was being shy to get closer to him at homecoming during a slow dance to "Perfect" by Ed Sheeran. Now, I've been thinking till this day like, damn, I should've talked to him more and gotten closer during that moment alone. It was a good five minutes since I was slow dancing with my friend at first—then she got him. I want to go back in time, just for that special moment of me and that one boy who will be unknown here. Afterwards, the night was sadly over and it was time to go home.

I was in the car with my cousin and *we were suddenly driving in the air like some future kind of thing. All of a sudden I saw that boy in the car next to us. Our eyes locked—I got out of the flying car. I yelled out his name so he could come to me. He came and we were just vibing. Clouds were light pink around us. We remade that moment of us slow dancing. The sky turned colorful to every beat. We ended the night by floating on the beautiful clouds.*

What Chicago Needs

Chicago needs me and I'm going to change it by making it safer and cutting down all the gun violence and any other violence. There will be no racism at all because it's causing so many problems. There will be a personal driver for everyone. The drivers will be robots. Also, everyone will have more privacy. No one will gain weight, so you can eat a lot of food and still won't gain weight. All traveling is free, so if you want to travel somewhere, there's no cost.

No one will have to deal with paying bills. There will be no more bills. The college you want to go to is free, instead of you having to save up money for college. You won't have to deal with paying your Netflix account monthly like you're supposed to.

Education would be free from now on, in my Chicago. There would be free makeup for us girls or boys who are willing to do their makeup. There will be makeup classes for anyone who is interested in makeup. One day, there will be free haircuts. The next day there will be free nails, etc.

The sky will be a nice purple and clouds will be black. Trees will be colorful and change every five minutes. Everyone gets a pet of their choice and the pets will never die.

Joining Chicago's Literary Tradition: An Afterword

by Rich Farrell

Washington High School is located in the East Side neighborhood. Skyscrapers sink to streets lined with bungalows. A neighborhood born of industry, complete with river ports, train tracks, and the Skyway, simultaneously link and divide. "L" tracks don't reach us. Streets are named by letter. We have a forest preserve complete with picnic groves and wildflowers. We face many of the same challenges as our neighbors to the north and west, but the resources set up around the city for our schools don't typically find their way here.

I initially reached out to 826CHI to try to develop an informal writing group for some of my students who were interested in writing but couldn't make it to the city center where many programs are centered. Instead, I was presented with the chance to bring programming to all students I teach through their Young Authors Book Project. Anyone who works with teens know that they have a lot to say. Being able to craft those voices and share ideas with a larger audience was better than expected.

Our curriculum focused around identity. We asked ourselves questions like "Who am I?" and "How does my understanding of myself help me contribute to my community and the larger world?" Our relationship to our community and city was central to our understandings of ourselves. Considering how our experiences shape and are shaped by our surroundings was natural. Thinking about how our surroundings could be shifted into something better and new, either real or imagined, was an exercise in hope and benevolence.

It wasn't always easy. There were times when students came in with their eyes glazed over with sleep, when ideas weren't fully formed, or when frustration set in because the words wouldn't come out just right and the task seemed too ambitious. There were also times where they gasped and their eyes grew wide listening to poems composed by Eve Ewing and José Olivarez and the energy of exploring and debating those ideas, laughed picking out images to create collages as a prewriting strategy, and sighed with contentment and satisfaction when their own pieces were completed. I had a chance to see some of my students who previously balked at writing create flowing paragraphs. I saw smiles lift the corners of lips like the expectations set with and for them. The process reminds me of lines from Hermann Hesse's Demian: "Was it only difficult? Wasn't it beautiful too?"

This collection is, among so many things, an exploration of what Chicago is, could, and should be. Reflecting on their pieces now, I can see how much of a pull the space has on its writers and philosophers. Although many of my students aren't familiar with Chicago's literary canon, they nevertheless channeled the sense of growth of Sandra Cisneros, the sense of community of Gwendolyn Brooks, the sense of gruff perseverance of Carl Sandburg, the rough-around-the-edges realities of Nelson Algren, and the outrage around class and race inequalities of Lorraine Hansberry and Richard Wright. Surely there's something special in the Chicago air that our young and old breathe alike, which generates gusts of change and gives new meaning to the nickname "The Windy City".

Curriculum Guide 2018-19

The Young Authors Book Project is a special yearly program at 826CHI. Its writing focus each year varies but the outcome is always a published book filled with the original words of the young people in Chicago. This year the project centered on the theme of a desire based narrative. Students were tasked with writing about the Chicago they want to see and want to live in. They tapped into their experiences, imaginations, dreams, and knowledge in order to envision what life could be like in a youth-centered, youth-powered, and youth-led Chicago.

This plan was designed to ignite imaginations and spark creativity while tackling big issues that affect our city. You will find that you can easily manipulate or supplement the content or standards to address younger and older students, following the ladder of the Common Core State Standards and your own expertise. Our hope in writing this guide is that you will be able to construct your own plans in conjunction with this work. You will also find, at the end, suggestions for using this text in your plans and classrooms.

Essential Questions

Essential Questions are those that guide our study throughout the year. By nature, they should be open-ended, and significant to your area of focus.

We chose the following Essential Questions:
1. How does living in Chicago impact how you live each day?
2. What is important to you about this city?
3. What are some issues you want resolved in this city? Why?
4. What does freedom and happiness for all mean?

Primary Readings, in order of our study

Suspending Damage: A Letter to Communities by Eve Tuck (essay: Harvard Educational Review, 2009)
This essay is the basis of the entire curriculum. Educators (and all readers) are encouraged to read this essay prior to implementing any lessons with students. Essay Here: *http://pages.ucsd.edu/~rfrank/class_web/ES-114A/Week%204/TuckHEdR79-3. pdf*

A Flower Blooming in the Dark (anthology: 826CHI, 2018)
An anthology of first-person narratives and poetry written by students attending three schools across the city of Chicago, this book was supported and produced by 826CHI. These short tales provide a jumping off point for student writing. They were developed to follow a strict narrative text structure, but are based in students' personal experiences. This is a powerful reading and provides great motivation for writing. See *www.826national.org* for writing resources and reading for yourself and your classroom.

Electric Arches by Eve L. Ewing (poetry: Haymarket Books, 2018)
In order to model how to blend real events with creative solutions we read Chicago-based poet, Eve Ewing's Re-tellings as mentor texts. Within these pieces Ewing places the reader in a memory in which power was in the hands of an oppressor. The memory is interrupted by the creation of a new ending where power shifts and the imagination takes over. Students were intrigued by the blending of fact and fantasy. The discussions centered on power, voice, and action in scary situations. Students reflected and wrote their own version of a re-telling based on a memory in which they wanted to re-write the ending.

Compendium 5 (anthology: 826CHI, 2016)
The 9th grade students were having some difficulty infusing their narratives with fantastical elements. We turned to younger student writing from this anthology that includes 1st grade-12th grade writers. Reading and seeing work from students in elementary school that was confidently full of silliness, imagination, and fantasy gave the 9th graders a new outlook on what writing can be.

Citizen Illegal **by José Olivarez (poetry: Haymarket Books, 2018)**
The major focus for our students with this collection was a particular poem titled "Mexican Heaven". Here Chicago-based poet, Olivarez creates a heaven that is based on Mexican culture and its people. Olivarez writes what is familiar to him - the heaven that he envisions based on his experience. This poem was the springboard for students to begin answering the biggest question of the project: What would Chicago look like if you were in charge - if Chicago was youth-centered and youth-driven?

Declaration **by Phillip B. Williams (poem: Chicago Magazine, 2015)**
Throughout the curriculum we centered Chicago-based writers to demonstrate to students the many ways Chicago is interpreted and the many voices/stories that make-up this city. Williams' poem is one we used to discuss what we love about our city but also what in our city loves us in return.

People and Organizations

Artist: **Titus Kaphar**
Titus is an American painter that recomposes art to include and center Black people. His art was inspiration for students to understand that the stories we hear are often centered in white adult voices in order to change that the students had to take charge of their own narrative and focus their experiences to be front and center. *https://www.kapharstudio.com/*

Artist: **Krista Franklin**
Krista is a poet and visual artist. Her work "emerges at the intersections poetics, popular culture, and the dynamic histories of the African Diaspora." We viewed and discussed her collages to illustrate that students could create new realities from existing elements. Students then created their own collages with the goal of establishing a visual representation of the Chicago they want to live in. *http://www.kristafranklin.com/*

Activities You Could Do With This Book (at home or in the classroom)

Add a New Ending:
Based on what has been written already, choose a stopping point and write a new ending. Another option would be to write multiple endings. Ask the writer(s) to imagine the creator making a different choice at some point, and then add as many endings as are possible.

Create a Graphic Representation/Collage of the Text:
Asking the reader(s) to interpret the text in graphic novel form, collage, or via photography is an interesting and interactive way to improve close reading skills and comprehension. You may allow for creative interpretation or ask creators to stick to the textual evidence. Either way, this type of activity is engaging on many levels, for a variety of learning styles.

Socratic Dialogue:
Young people love to be heard, and this kind of discussion allows everyone to have a well-prepared voice. Ask readers to read the same piece and take a stand or make a claim about how this version of Chicago serves its people. What could alter the frame of the experience? Are there legal issues? Ask students to annotate the piece with these or other questions in mind. In the following days, engage students in a regulated discussion of the story, with textual evidence as their main frame of reference and allow research to support their claims.

Questioning the Author:
There are many ways to address an author. If you could give them advice, support, a third person omniscient view of their experience, what would you—could you—say to them? If you could interview them what would you ask?

Use Any Piece as an Introduction:
Imagine any piece you choose is just the background or flashback of a protagonist. How would the story move forward? What choices would a character in this environment make going forward in life?

Write a Response Story:
Ask writers to choose a favorite piece, or choose one for a whole group. Many of the pieces in this book are based on what would be best for the writer. Have your students think and respond to the environment - is it also good to them? Would they also benefit from being in this version of Chicago? If yes, how? If not, how and what would they change to also benefit?

Build Your Own:
Have students begin to imagine a Chicago in which they are the leaders. What does the city look like? What do the people do? How do they ensure freedom and happiness for all? This can be a written or visual piece. Option to give students more or less structure - should they weave in elements of fantasy? Should they only be realistic?

Create a Leadership Guide:
Ask students to focus on one main issue from a piece in the book or find an issue that they deem important in Chicago. Have them create a how-to or instructional manual on how leaders should be handling the situation.

Manifesto:
Students begin by listing their skills, passions, beliefs, and any injustices they want to address. Have students arrange their lists to create a poem or they could use the lists as inspiration for a poem where each line begins with, "I believe..."

Black Out:
Ask writers to choose a favorite piece or choose one for the whole group. Provide a copy of the piece to each student along with a black marker and a pencil. Have the students silently scan the page for any word(s) that stand out or catch their attention. Students should draw a box around their chosen word. Then read the piece as a whole class. Students should focus on finding other words that relate/connect to the word in the box. Let students begin to cross out any words or phrases in the piece they don't want. The remaining words create a new piece of work. Option to have students design or draw on the piece to make their blackout poem stand out.

Reflection

Using the questions listed here, reflect on a specific story or the text as a whole:

1. Regarding the re-tellings: Have there been moments or situations in your life that you wish you had handled differently? Have you ever imagined going back in time to say the thing you didn't say in an argument? What's the driving force behind that feeling?
2. Many of the pieces in this anthology feature difficult situations or subject matter, yet manage to be inspiring and uplifting. Reflect on why you as a reader felt uplifted or inspired. How was the writer able to accomplish this?
3. Which stories did you find most affecting? What particular stories kept crossing your mind after reading the entire book?
4. What are the issues that affect you most living in your community or city? What would you do to make life better for everyone if you were the leader of that place?

Common Core Alignment

All Common Core State Language Arts Standards could be addressed in this plan of study. You may access all the standards at *www.corestandards. org*. We also incorporated the WIDA Standards to accommodate English Language Learners. You may access those standards at *www.wida.us/ standards*. We chose to focus on the following:

Reading Literature

CCSS.ELA-LITERACY.RL.9-10.1
Cite strong and thorough textual evidence to support analysis of what the text says explicitly as well as inferences drawn from the text.

CCSS.ELA-LITERACY.RL.9-10.2
Determine a theme or central idea of a text and analyze in detail its development over the course of the text, including how it emerges and is shaped and refined by specific details; provide an objective summary of the text.

CCSS.ELA-LITERACY.RL.9-10.5
Analyze how an author's choices concerning how to structure a text, order events within it (e.g., parallel plots), and manipulate time (e.g., pacing, flashbacks) create such effects as mystery, tension, or surprise.

CCSS.ELA-LITERACY.RL.9-10.9
Analyze how an author draws on and transforms source material in a specific work (e.g., how Shakespeare treats a theme or topic from Ovid or the Bible or how a later author draws on a play by Shakespeare).

Reading Informational Text

CCSS.ELA-LITERACY.RI.9-10.5
Analyze in detail how an author's ideas or claims are developed and refined by particular sentences, paragraphs, or larger portions of a text (e.g., a section or chapter).

CCSS.ELA-LITERACY.RI.9-10.6
Determine an author's point of view or purpose in a text and analyze how an author uses rhetoric to advance that point of view or purpose.

CCSS.ELA-LITERACY.RI.9-10.7
Analyze various accounts of a subject told in different mediums (e.g., a person's life story in both print and multimedia), determining which details are emphasized in each account.

Writing

CCSS.ELA-LITERACY.W.9-10.2
Write informative/explanatory texts to examine and convey complex ideas, concepts, and information clearly and accurately through the effective selection, organization, and analysis of content.

CCSS.ELA-LITERACY.W.9-10.3
Write narratives to develop real or imagined experiences or events using effective technique, well-chosen details, and well-structured event sequences.

CCSS.ELA-LITERACY.W.9-10.4
Produce clear and coherent writing in which the development, organization, and style are appropriate to task, purpose, and audience. (Grade-specific expectations for writing types are defined in standards 1-3 above.)

CCSS.ELA-LITERACY.W.9-10.5
Develop and strengthen writing as needed by planning, revising, editing,

rewriting, or trying a new approach, focusing on addressing what is most significant for a specific purpose and audience. (Editing for conventions should demonstrate command of Language standards 1-3 up to and including grades 9-10 here.)

CCSS.ELA-LITERACY.W.9-10.6

Use technology, including the Internet, to produce, publish, and update individual or shared writing products, taking advantage of technology's capacity to link to other information and to display information flexibly and dynamically.

CCSS.ELA-LITERACY.W.9-10.7

Conduct short as well as more sustained research projects to answer a question (including a self-generated question) or solve a problem; narrow or broaden the inquiry when appropriate; synthesize multiple sources on the subject, demonstrating understanding of the subject under investigation.

CCSS.ELA-LITERACY.W.9-10.9

Draw evidence from literary or informational texts to support analysis, reflection, and research.

CCSS.ELA-LITERACY.W.9-10.10

Write routinely over extended time frames (time for research, reflection, and revision) and shorter time frames (a single sitting or a day or two) for a range of tasks, purposes, and audiences.

Speaking and Listening

CCSS.ELA-LITERACY.SL.9-10.1

Initiate and participate effectively in a range of collaborative discussions (one-on-one, in groups, and teacher-led) with diverse partners on grades 9-10 topics, texts, and issues, building on others' ideas and expressing their own clearly and persuasively.

CCSS.ELA-LITERACY.SL.9-10.2
Integrate multiple sources of information presented in diverse media or formats (e.g., visually, quantitatively, orally) evaluating the credibility and accuracy of each source.

CCSS.ELA-LITERACY.SL.9-10.3
Evaluate a speaker's point of view, reasoning, and use of evidence and rhetoric, identifying any fallacious reasoning or exaggerated or distorted evidence.

CCSS.ELA-LITERACY.SL.9-10.4
Present information, findings, and supporting evidence clearly, concisely, and logically such that listeners can follow the line of reasoning and the organization, development, substance, and style are appropriate to purpose, audience, and task.

CCSS.ELA-LITERACY.SL.9-10.5
Make strategic use of digital media (e.g., textual, graphical, audio, visual, and interactive elements) in presentations to enhance understanding of findings, reasoning, and evidence and to add interest.

Language

CCSS.ELA-LITERACY.L.9-10.2
Demonstrate command of the conventions of standard English capitalization, punctuation, and spelling when writing.

CCSS.ELA-LITERACY.L.9-10.3
Apply knowledge of language to understand how language functions in different contexts, to make effective choices for meaning or style, and to comprehend more fully when reading or listening.

CCSS.ELA-LITERACY.L.9-10.4
Determine or clarify the meaning of unknown and multiple-meaning words and phrases based on grades 9-10 reading and content, choosing flexibly from a range of strategies.

Acknowledgments

We are incredibly grateful for the generosity of our donors, who fund our programs and publications. Thank you for giving our students the opportunity to become published authors and share their stories with the world. You help them creatively engage with their community, enriching the lives of their families, teachers, and peers throughout our city. This publication was made possible in part by the Donley Foundation, the Chauncey and Marion D. McCormick Family Foundation, the Porsche Club of America—Chicago Region, the James & Brenda S. Grusecki Family Foundation, Jackson National Community Fund, Pelino Charitable Foundation, Elizabeth Morse Genius Trust, Crown Family Philanthropies, The Judy Family Foundation, the Kathleen Evans Household, Gillian Flynn and Brett Nolan, Justine Jentes and Dan Kuruna, Christine and Thomas Quinn, and Shawn Clark.

This project would not exist without the hard work of the students, teachers, and administrators at George Washington High School. Rich Farrell, you're a marvel of patience and thoughtfulness and we're in awe of the passion with which you advocate for your students. We'd like to give a hearty round of applause to the brave students who shared their ideas with us and from whom we can learn so much. Extra claps for the student ambassadors who contributed to the student foreword: Jose, Laisha, Benjamin, Isabella, and Andrew.

A million and one thank you's to Grace Molteni, whose clever, playful, and stunning cover design brought this book to life. Wendy Robles took our students' words and created a thoughtful, attentive, and flawless layout that enables their work to stand out. José Olivarez managed to step away from his own incredible work to write a phenomenal foreword that highlights and champions the work in this book. Thank you, José! We can't wait to enjoy what you write next!

Our warmest thanks to Natasha Mijares and Cherish Harber who gave their time to aid students with the writing process. Thank you to the cohort of copy editors for this book: Clayton Crook, Luke Gerwe, Maya Odim, and Jill Quarles who ensured that each students' voice got the right amount of polish to truly shine through.

The intern cohort of 2018-2019 are astoundingly talented, intelligent, big-hearted, and hard-working. This project would not have existed without their commitment and skill. Thank you, thank you, thank you to Madi Casteel, Emily Coffee, Clayton Crook, Monet Foster, Taylor Fustin, Mandy Grathwohl, Cherish Harber, Gaga Li, Emily Lien, Enrique Orosco, Julia Pappageorge, and Kate Walton.

Finally, thank you, reader, for picking up this book of student writing. We hope you see the value in listening to young people who can see the world around them and provide fresh perspective on how we could all improve. They provided the dreams; it is only together that we can make some of them a reality.

More Books from 826CHI

Submerged in Euphoria
Pitchfork Music Writing Intensive

The Five Senses of Home // Los Cinco Sentidos del Hogar
After-School Tutoring & Writing, Spring 2019

We Are Worth More Than the Universe
Workshops Anthology, 2018

In A World Far, Far Away
After-School Tutoring & Writing, Fall 2018

Compendium, Volume 6
Anthology, 2018

A Flower Blooming in the Dark
Young Authors Book Project, 2018

I Will Hold You Like a Bible
Teen Writers Studio, 2018

**But I Am Myself and I Am Perfect for it //
Pero yo soy yo mismo y soy perfecto por eso**
After-School Tutoring & Writing, Spring 2018

The Moon Wrote a Song
After-School Tutoring & Writing, Fall 2017

P.S. You Sound Like Someone I Can Trust
Young Authors Book Project, 2017

About 826CHI

826CHI ("eight-two-six Chicago") is a nonprofit organization dedicated to supporting students ages six to 18 with their creative and expository writing skills, and to helping teachers inspire their students to write. Our services are structured around the understanding that great leaps in learning can happen with individualized attention, and that strong writing skills are fundamental to future success.

With this in mind, we provide after-school tutoring, creative writing workshops, in-school residencies, field trips, support for English Language Learners, and publishing opportunities for Chicago youth—all at absolutely no cost to Chicago's schools, teachers, and students.

We strive for all of our programs to strengthen each student's power to express ideas effectively, creatively, confidently, and in their individual voice by providing them a safe space to be their most creative selves. Learn more at: *www.826chi.org.*

About the Wicker Park Secret Agent Supply Co.

826CHI shares its space with the Wicker Park Secret Agent Supply Co., a store with a not-so-secret mission. Our unique products encourage creative writing and imaginative play, and trigger new adventures for agents of all ages. Every purchase supports 826CHI's free programming, so visit us at 1276 N Milwaukee Ave in Wicker Park to pick up writing tools, fancy notebooks, assorted fake moustaches and other stellar disguises, books from local publishers, our latest student publications, and much more!

Or, visit us online at: *www.secretagentsupply.com.*

Our Programs

826CHI's free programs reach students at every opportunity—in school, after school, in the evenings, and on the weekends.

After-School Tutoring and Writing
826CHI is packed four afternoons a week with students in first through eighth grade working on their homework and sharpening their creative writing skills. Volunteer tutors help students with any and all homework assignments and lead students in daily creative and expository writing activities. Student writing created during tutoring is published in chapbooks throughout the year, and we frequently host student readings for parents, tutors, families, and the greater 826CHI community.

Field Trips
On weekday mornings throughout the school year, we host classes from Chicago schools for lively, writing-based Field Trips at our writing center. Teachers may choose from a wide range of programs, such as our Storytelling & Bookmaking Field Trip, which focuses on plot and character development, or "I Remember . . ." Memoir Writing, in which teenage students transform powerful memories into reflective prose.

In-School Partnerships
Because it can be difficult for teachers and students to make it to our center during the school day, 826CHI brings itself into schools across the city. Thanks to our dedicated volunteer pool, we're able to bring a team writing coaches to give individualized attention to students as they tackle various projects. Do you have an idea for a writing project and could use the assistance of 826CHI's educators and volunteers?

Workshops

Designed to foster creativity, strengthen writing skills, and provide students with a forum to execute projects they otherwise might not have the support to undertake, 826CHI Workshops are led by talented volunteers—including published authors, educators, playwrights, chefs, and other artists—during the school year and throughout the summer.

Teen Writers Studio

826CHI's Teen Writers Studio (or "TWS") is a year-long creative writing workshop that connects high school students to fellow writers, including peers and older professionals in the field. It's open to anyone in 9th-12th grade and welcomes youth from all over the city. TWS members meet twice each month to write together, talk about writing, and produce a literary chapbook each June. If you're into any of the above, this space is for you.

Publishing

At 826CHI, each student is challenged to produce their finest writing, knowing that their words will have the opportunity to be read, laughed at, wept over, or deeply pondered by their family, friends, and folks they may not even know. By the power of a very heavy binding machine, we are able to assemble many of the students' pieces into handsome books in-house. When not laying out, cutting up, and binding at 826CHI, we send special collections of writing (like this one!) to a professional printer with gigantic machines in order to put together a well-bound publication.

826CHI Staff

Kendra Curry-Khanna; *Executive Director*

Julia Clausen; *Data and Impact Associate, Americorps VISTA*

Ola Faleti; *Development Coordinator*

Molly Fannin; *Director of Development*

Gaby FeBland; *Communications Coordinator*

Gerardo Galán; *Program Coordinator*

Waringa Hunja; *Publications Coordinator*

Mackenzie Lynch; *Communications Associate, Americorps VISTA*

Natasha Mijares; *Program and Evaluation Manager*

Nire Nah; *Retail Associate*

David Pintor; *Volunteer Manager*

Molly Sprayregen; *Program Coordinator*

Tyler Stoltenberg; *Operations Manager*

Maria Villarreal; *Director of Programs*